gratins
& bakes

Women's Weekly THE AUSTRALIAN

CONTENTS

AUSTRALIAN CUP AND SPOON MEASUREMENTS ARE METRIC. A CONVERSION CHART APPEARS ON PAGE 77.

Gratins and bakes are the ultimate comfort food. These always-popular dishes are both perfect for the family and entertaining – you can do all the preparation beforehand and just reheat when it's time to serve. Nothing could be easier, or more delicious.

Pamela Clark

Food Director

WINTER VEGETABLE GRATIN

prep & cook time 1¼ hours **serves** 4 **nutritional count per serving** 13.9g total fat (8.7g saturated fat); 1810kJ (433 cal); 57.6g carbohydrate; 19.1g protein; 8.8g fibre

3 medium potatoes (600g)
1 large swede (450g)
1 large kumara (500g)
2 medium carrots (240g)
½ cup (35g) stale breadcrumbs
¾ cup (60g) finely grated parmesan cheese
white sauce
40g butter
¼ cup (35g) plain flour
2 cups (500ml) skim milk
pinch ground nutmeg

1 Preheat oven to 200°C/180°C fan-forced. Oil deep 19cm-square cake pan.
2 Make white sauce.
3 Using sharp knife, mandoline or V-slicer, slice vegetables thinly; pat dry with absorbent paper.
4 Layer potato slices in prepared pan; pour a third of the white sauce over potato slices. Layer carrot, another a third of the white sauce, then swede, remaining white sauce and finally the kumara. Cover; bake about 1½ hours or until vegetables are tender. Uncover, top kumara with combined breadcrumbs and cheese; bake, uncovered, about 20 minutes or until top is browned lightly. Stand 10 minutes before serving.
white sauce Melt butter in medium saucepan; add flour; cook, stirring, 1 minute. Remove from heat, gradually stir in milk; return to heat. Cook, stirring, until sauce boils and thickens. Stir in nutmeg; season to taste.

GRATINS

creamed spinach, kumara and potato gratin

CREAMED SPINACH, KUMARA AND POTATO GRATIN

prep & cook time 1¾ hours serves 6 nutritional count per serving 26.7g total fat (16.9g saturated fat); 1655kJ (396 cal); 27.6g carbohydrate; 9.2g protein; 5.7g fibre

10g butter
1 teaspoon olive oil
1 medium brown onion (150g), chopped finely
2 x 250g packets frozen spinach, thawed, drained
300ml cream
¾ cup (180ml) milk
1 large kumara (500g), sliced thinly
2 large potatoes (600g), sliced thinly
⅓ cup (25g) grated parmesan cheese

1 Preheat oven to 220°C/200°C fan-forced. Oil deep 25cm x 30cm baking dish.
2 Melt butter with oil in frying pan; cook onion until soft. Add spinach, ½ cup of the cream and ½ cup of the milk; cook, stirring, 2 minutes.
3 Place a third of the kumara and a third of the potato, slightly overlapping, in dish; spread with half the spinach mixture. Repeat layering, ending with kumara and potato. Pour over remaining combined cream and milk; sprinkle with cheese.
4 Bake, covered, in oven, about 1 hour or until potato is tender. Uncover; bake about a further 10 minutes or until browned lightly.

PASTITSIO

prep & cook time 2¼ hours serves 6 nutritional count per serving 45.8g total fat (22.7g saturated fat); 3528kJ (844 cal); 52.5g carbohydrate; 52.1g protein; 4.1g fibre

250g macaroni pasta
2 eggs, beaten lightly
¾ cup (60g) grated parmesan cheese
2 tablespoons stale breadcrumbs
meat sauce
2 tablespoons olive oil
2 medium brown onions (300g), chopped finely
750g beef mince
400g can crushed tomatoes
⅓ cup (90g) tomato paste
½ cup (125ml) beef stock
¼ cup (60ml) dry white wine
½ teaspoon ground cinnamon
1 egg, beaten lightly

pastitsio

cheese topping
90g butter
½ cup (75g) plain flour
3½ cups (875ml) milk
1 cup (80g) grated parmesan cheese
2 egg yolks

1 Preheat oven to 180°C/160°C fan-forced. Oil shallow 2.5-litre (10-cup) ovenproof dish.
2 Make meat sauce; make cheese topping.
3 Cook pasta in large saucepan of boiling water until tender. Drain, then combine with egg and cheese in large bowl; press over base of dish.
4 Top pasta with meat sauce; pour over cheese topping then sprinkle with breadcrumbs. Bake, in oven, about 1 hour or until browned lightly.
meat sauce Heat oil in pan; cook onion and beef until browned. Stir in undrained tomatoes, paste, stock, wine and cinnamon; simmer, uncovered, 20 minutes or until mixture is thick. Cool 10 minutes, then stir in egg.
cheese topping Melt butter in pan, add flour; cook until mixture bubbles and thickens. Remove from heat; gradually stir in milk. Stir over heat until sauce boils and thickens; stir in cheese. Cool 5 minutes, then stir in egg yolks.

italian cottage pie

ITALIAN COTTAGE PIE

prep & cook time 1½ hours serves 6 nutritional count
per serving 19.4g total fat (8.8g saturated fat); 2040kJ
(488 cal); 37.1g carbohydrate; 37.5g protein; 6.7g fibre

1 tablespoon olive oil
1 medium brown onion (150g), chopped finely
2 cloves garlic, crushed
200g large button mushrooms, sliced thinly
1 large carrot (180g), diced into 1cm pieces
1 medium eggplant (300g), diced into cubes
750g lamb mince
1 tablespoon plain flour
½ cup (125ml) dry red wine
425g can crushed tomatoes
2 tablespoons tomato paste
1 tablespoon worcestershire sauce
2 tablespoons finely chopped fresh oregano
800g potatoes, chopped coarsely
20g butter
⅓ cup (80ml) milk
¼ cup (20g) grated parmesan cheese
soft polenta
1¼ cups (310ml) chicken stock
¾ cup (180ml) milk
½ cup (85g) polenta
¼ cup (20g) grated parmesan cheese

1 Preheat oven to 200°C/180°C fan-forced.
Oil deep 2.5-litre (10-cup) casserole dish.
2 Heat oil in large frying pan; cook onion, garlic,
mushrooms, carrot and eggplant, stirring, until
onion softens. Add lamb; cook until browned.
Add flour; cook 1 minute. Add wine; bring to the
boil, stirring. Stir in undrained tomatoes, paste,
sauce and oregano. Simmer, uncovered, about
10 minutes or until mixture thickens slightly.
3 Meanwhile, make soft polenta.
4 Cook potato until tender, drain; mash with
butter and milk until smooth. Gently swirl hot
polenta mixture into potato mixture.
5 Spoon mince mixture into dish; top with
polenta mixture, sprinkle with cheese. Bake, in
oven, 25 minutes or until cheese browns lightly.
soft polenta Combine stock and milk in pan;
bring to the boil. Gradually add polenta, stirring
constantly. Reduce heat; cook, stirring, about
10 minutes or until thickened. Stir in cheese.

MACARONI CHEESE

prep & cook time 1 hour serves 4 nutritional count
per serving 47.5g total fat (27.8g saturated fat); 3854kJ
(922 cal); 78.8g carbohydrate; 43.1g protein; 3.5g fibre

300g macaroni pasta
4 rindless bacon rashers (260g), chopped finely
50g butter
⅓ cup (50g) plain flour
1 litre (4 cups) milk
1 cup (120g) grated cheddar cheese
½ cup (40g) grated pecorino cheese
2 tablespoons wholegrain mustard
½ cup (35g) stale breadcrumbs
20g butter, extra

1 Preheat oven to 180°C/160°C fan-forced.
Oil deep 2-litre (8-cup) ovenproof dish.
2 Cook pasta in large saucepan of boiling water
until tender; drain.
3 Cook bacon in medium pan until crisp; drain.
4 Melt butter in pan; cook flour, stirring, 1 minute.
Stir in milk; cook until sauce boils and thickens.
Cool 2 minutes; stir in cheeses and mustard.
5 Combine pasta, sauce and bacon in large
bowl. Pour mixture into ovenproof dish; top
with breadcrumbs, dot with extra butter. Bake,
in oven, about 30 minutes or until browned.

macaroni cheese

fish pie with caper rösti topping

FISH PIE WITH CAPER RÖSTI TOPPING

prep & cook time **35 minutes** serves **4** nutritional count per serving 23.4g total fat (14.8g saturated fat); 1910kJ (457 cal); 23g carbohydrate; 37.3g protein; 3g fibre

100g uncooked small prawns
600g firm white fish fillets, chopped coarsely
¼ cup (35g) plain flour
25g butter
½ cup (120g) sour cream
½ cup (60g) frozen peas
¼ cup coarsely chopped fresh dill
caper rösti topping
500g potatoes, peeled, grated coarsely
2 tablespoons rinsed drained baby capers
25g butter, melted

1 Make caper rösti topping.
2 Shell and devein prawns. Coat seafood in flour; shake off excess. Heat butter in frying pan; cook seafood, in batches, for 3 minutes. Return seafood to pan with sour cream, peas and dill; cook, stirring occasionally, about 5 minutes or until seafood is cooked through.
3 Preheat grill. Spread seafood into shallow 2.5-litre (10-cup) ovenproof dish; top with caper rösti mixture. Grill about 10 minutes or until topping is tender and golden brown.
caper rösti topping Squeeze excess moisture from potato; combine with capers and butter in medium bowl.

CHICKPEA & VEGETABLE GRATIN

prep & cook time **1 hour** serves **6** nutritional count per serving 13.3g total fat (3.9g saturated fat); 1296kJ (310 cal); 26.4g carbohydrate; 15.8g protein; 11.2g fibre

2 tablespoons olive oil
1 brown onion (200g), chopped finely
4 cloves garlic, crushed
½ teaspoon ground allspice
½ teaspoon chilli flakes
2 x 400g cans diced tomatoes
2 red capsicums (700g)
2 eggplants (600g), cut into 5mm slices
3 zucchini (360g), cut into 5mm slices
2 x 400g cans chickpeas, rinsed, drained

chickpea & vegetable gratin

½ cup chopped fresh flat-leaf parsley
⅓ cup chopped fresh basil
1 teaspoon fresh thyme leaves
1 teaspoon white sugar
1 cup (80g) grated parmesan cheese

1 Heat half the oil in saucepan; cook onion, stirring, until softened. Add garlic, allspice and chilli; cook, stirring, until fragrant. Add undrained tomatoes; simmer, uncovered, about 15 minutes or until sauce thickens slightly.
2 Quarter capsicums; discard seeds and membranes. Roast under preheated hot grill, skin-side up, until skin blisters and blackens. Cover with plastic wrap for 5 minutes; peel away skin then cut capsicum into 3cm pieces.
3 Combine eggplant, zucchini and remaining oil in large bowl; place vegetables on two oven trays, grill both sides until tender.
4 Preheat oven to 200°C/180°C fan-forced.
5 Stir chickpeas, herbs and sugar into tomato sauce. Place half the combined capsicum, eggplant and zucchini in shallow 2.5-litre (10-cup) ovenproof dish; pour half the chickpea sauce over vegetables. Repeat layering; sprinkle with cheese. Bake, uncovered, in oven, about 20 minutes or until browned lightly.

eggplant parmigiana

one-third of the cheeses and one-third of the oregano. Repeat layering.

6 Bake, covered, in oven, 20 minutes. Uncover; bake about 10 minutes or until browned lightly.

COQUILLES SAINT JACQUES

prep & cook time **45 minutes** serves **4** nutritional count per serving **38.8g total fat (23.5g saturated fat); 2558kJ (612 cal); 21.1g carbohydrate; 33.9g protein; 2.7g fibre**

1½ cups (375ml) chicken stock
1 cup (250ml) dry white wine
2 shallots (50g), chopped finely
750g scallops, without roe
250g button mushrooms, sliced thinly
50g butter
2 tablespoons plain flour
½ cup (125ml) milk
½ cup (125ml) cream
2 egg yolks
2 teaspoons lemon juice
1 cup (70g) stale breadcrumbs
2 tablespoons grated swiss cheese
1 tablespoon chopped fresh chives
30g butter, extra, melted

1 Boil stock, wine and shallots in medium pan; reduce heat. Add scallops and mushrooms; simmer until scallops are barely cooked. Remove from liquid with a slotted spoon.
2 Boil liquid 5 minutes or until reduced to ½ cup. Strain into heatproof bowl; reserve liquid.
3 Melt butter in pan; cook flour, stirring, until mixture thickens. Stir in combined milk, cream and reserved liquid. Cook until mixture boils and thickens. Remove from heat; whisk in egg yolks and juice. Season to taste.
4 Combine breadcrumbs, cheese, chives and extra butter in medium bowl. Divide scallops and mushrooms among four 1-cup (250ml) gratin dishes; spoon over sauce. Sprinkle with breadcrumb mixture. Cook scallops under a preheated grill until browned lightly.

EGGPLANT PARMIGIANA

prep & cook time **1 hour** serves **6** nutritional count per serving **27.7g total fat (6.6g saturated fat); 2266kJ (542 cal); 49.4g carbohydrate; 19.9g protein; 8.3g fibre**

2 large eggplants (1kg)
vegetable oil, for shallow-frying
½ cup (75g) plain flour
4 eggs, beaten lightly
2 cups (200g) packaged breadcrumbs
3 cups (750g) bottled tomato pasta sauce
1 cup (100g) grated mozzarella cheese
¼ cup (20g) grated parmesan cheese
⅓ cup loosely packed fresh oregano leaves

1 Using vegetable peeler, peel random strips of skin from eggplants; discard skins. Slice eggplants thinly.
2 Heat oil in large frying pan.
3 Coat eggplant in flour; shake off excess. Dip in egg, then in breadcrumbs. Shallow-fry eggplant, in batches, until browned lightly. Drain on absorbent paper.
4 Preheat oven to 200°C/180°C fan-forced.
5 Spread about one-third of the pasta sauce over base of oiled 2.5-litre (10-cup) ovenproof dish. Top with about one-third of the eggplant,

coquilles Saint Jacques

lemon tuna mornay with peas

LEMON TUNA MORNAY WITH PEAS

prep & cook time **45 minutes** serves **6** nutritional count per serving **20.6g total fat (12.4g saturated fat); 2424kJ (580 cal); 62g carbohydrate; 33.9g protein; 4.1g fibre**

375g macaroni pasta
40g butter
¼ cup (35g) plain flour
2½ cups (625ml) skim milk, warmed
425g can tuna in spring water, drained, flaked
1 cup (120g) frozen peas
3 shallots (75g), chopped finely
1 tablespoon finely chopped fresh
　flat-leaf parsley
2 teaspoons finely grated lemon rind
2 tablespoons lemon juice
1 cup (120g) coarsely grated cheddar cheese
1 cup (70g) stale breadcrumbs
40g butter, chopped finely, extra

1 Preheat oven to 180°C/160°C fan-forced. Oil six 1½-cup (375ml) ovenproof dishes.
2 Cook pasta in large saucepan of boiling water until tender; drain.
3 Melt butter in medium saucepan, add flour; cook, stirring, until mixture bubbles and thickens. Gradually stir in milk; cook, stirring, until sauce boils and thickens. Combine sauce, tuna, peas, shallot, parsley, rind, juice and pasta in large bowl; season to taste.
4 Spoon pasta mixture into dishes; sprinkle with combined cheese and breadcrumbs, dollop with extra butter. Bake 30 minutes or until browned lightly. Stand 5 minutes before serving.

CASSOULET

prep & cook time **2½ hours (+ standing)** serves **6** nutritional count per serving **27.1g total fat (10.2g saturated fat); 2746kJ (657 cal); 40.4g carbohydrate; 56.7g protein; 12.4g fibre**

1½ cups (300g) dried white beans
300g boned pork belly, rind removed,
　sliced thinly
150g piece streaky bacon, rind removed,
　diced into 1cm pieces
800g piece boned lamb shoulder, diced
　into 3cm pieces

cassoulet

1 large brown onion (200g), chopped finely
1 small leek (200g), sliced thinly
2 cloves garlic, crushed
3 sprigs fresh thyme
400g can crushed tomatoes
2 bay leaves
1 cup (250ml) water
1 cup (250ml) chicken stock
2 cups (140g) stale breadcrumbs
⅓ cup chopped fresh flat-leaf parsley

1 Place beans in bowl, cover with water; stand overnight, drain. Rinse under cold water; drain. Place beans in saucepan of boiling water; return to the boil. Simmer, covered, about 15 minutes or until beans are just tender. Drain.
2 Preheat oven to 160°C/140°C fan-forced.
3 Cook pork in heated large flameproof casserole dish until browned; remove from dish. Cook bacon until crisp; remove from dish. Cook lamb, in batches, until browned; remove from dish.
4 Cook onion, leek and garlic in dish until onion softens. Add thyme, undrained tomatoes, bay leaves, the water, stock, beans and meat; bring to the boil. Cover; bake in oven 45 minutes. Uncover; sprinkle with combined breadcrumbs and parsley. Bake about 45 minutes or until liquid is nearly absorbed and beans are tender.

LAMB CASSOULET

prep & cook time 2¼ hours (+ standing) serves 4
nutritional count per serving 44.3g total fat
(13.9g saturated fat); 3603kJ (862 cal);
58g carbohydrate; 57.3g protein; 15.1g fibre

1 cup (200g) dried white beans
150g piece streaky bacon, rind removed,
    diced into 1cm pieces
500g thin lamb sausages, sliced thickly
1 medium brown onion (150g), chopped finely
2 trimmed celery stalks (200g), chopped finely
2 cloves garlic, crushed
1 sprig fresh rosemary
2 bay leaves
425g can crushed tomatoes
1½ cups (375ml) chicken stock
2 cups (140g) stale breadcrumbs
⅓ cup chopped fresh flat-leaf parsley
herb and rocket salad
60g baby rocket leaves
1 cup fresh flat-leaf parsley leaves
1 cup fresh chervil sprigs
½ cup fresh basil leaves
¼ cup (60ml) olive oil
2 tablespoons red wine vinegar
1 teaspoon white sugar

1 Place beans in bowl, cover with water; stand overnight, drain. Rinse under cold water; drain. Place beans in saucepan of boiling water; return to the boil. Reduce heat; simmer, covered, about 15 minutes or until beans are just tender. Drain.
2 Preheat oven to 160°C/140°C fan-forced.
3 Cook bacon in large flameproof casserole dish, on stove top, over high heat, pressing down with back of a spoon, until browned all over; remove from dish. Cook sausage in same dish until browned all over; remove from dish.
4 Cook onion, celery and garlic in same dish, stirring, about 5 minutes or until soft. Add rosemary, bay leaves, undrained tomatoes, stock, beans, bacon and sausage; bring to the boil. Cover; bake in oven 30 minutes. Remove from oven; sprinkle with combined breadcrumbs and parsley. Return to oven; bake, covered, 30 minutes. Uncover; bake about 10 minutes or until top browns lightly.
5 Meanwhile, make herb and rocket salad.
6 Toss salad with vinaigrette just before serving with cassoulet.

herb and rocket salad Combine rocket, parsley, chervil and basil in large bowl. Place remaining ingredients in screw-top jar; shake vinaigrette well.

notes There are many regional variations of French cassoulet; ours is based on a traditional Toulousaine version. We used white haricot beans in this recipe, but navy, great northern, cannellini or even lima beans can be used if you prefer.

vegetable ratatouille

VEGETABLE RATATOUILLE

prep & cook time 2¼ hours serves 6 nutritional count
per serving 24.7g total fat (9.1g saturated fat); 2090kJ
(500 cal); 43.9g carbohydrate, 22.1g protein, 12.7g fibre

800g celeriac, trimmed, chopped coarsely
2 large carrots (360g), chopped coarsely
2 medium parsnips (500g), chopped coarsely
2 medium kumara (800g), chopped coarsely
⅓ cup (80ml) olive oil
1 large brown onion (200g), chopped finely
3 cloves garlic, crushed
¼ cup loosely packed fresh oregano leaves
1 tablespoon tomato paste
2 x 425g cans crushed tomatoes
½ cup (125ml) dry red wine
1 cup (250ml) water
½ cup (40g) grated parmesan cheese
2½ cups (250g) grated mozzarella cheese
1 cup (70g) stale breadcrumbs
2 teaspoons finely grated lemon rind
½ cup chopped fresh flat-leaf parsley
2 tablespoons chopped fresh oregano

1 Preheat oven to 220°C/200°C fan-forced.
2 Combine celeriac, carrot, parsnip, kumara
and half the oil in large deep baking dish. Roast
about 50 minutes or until vegetables are tender
and browned lightly, stirring once, about halfway
through cooking time.
3 Heat remaining oil in large pan on stove
top; cook onion, garlic and oregano leaves until
onion softens. Add paste; cook 1 minute. Add
undrained tomatoes, wine and the water; boil,
uncovered, 10 minutes.
4 Add tomato mixture to vegetables in dish;
toss gently. Sprinkle with combined cheeses,
breadcrumbs, rind, parsley and chopped
oregano. Bake, in oven, about 20 minutes or
until top browns lightly.

RIGATONI WITH HERB CRUMB

prep & cook time 1¼ hours serves 6 nutritional count
per serving 18g total fat (9.1g saturated fat); 2353kJ
(563 cal); 65.7g carbohydrate; 30.8g protein; 6.2g fibre

30g butter
1 medium brown onion (150g), chopped finely

rigatoni with herb crumb

1 clove garlic, crushed
1 medium carrot (120g), chopped finely
500g beef mince
1 cup (250ml) milk
3 cups (750g) bottled tomato pasta sauce
375g rigatoni pasta
⅔ cup (70g) pizza cheese
½ cup (35g) stale breadcrumbs
2 teaspoons finely grated lemon rind
2 tablespoons chopped fresh flat-leaf parsley

1 Melt butter in large pan, add onion, garlic
and carrot; cook, stirring, until onion softens.
Add beef; cook, stirring, until browned. Add
milk; cook, stirring occasionally, until liquid
reduces by half. Add sauce; simmer, uncovered,
about 30 minutes or until sauce thickens.
2 Meanwhile, cook pasta in large saucepan
of boiling water until tender; drain.
3 Preheat oven to 220°C/200°C. Oil 2.5-litre
(10-cup) ovenproof dish.
4 Stir pasta and cheese into beef mixture;
spoon into dish. Sprinkle with combined
breadcrumbs, rind and parsley. Bake, in oven,
uncovered, about 30 minutes or until browned
lightly. Stand 10 minutes before serving.

ZUCCHINI GRATIN

prep & cook time 50 minutes serves 6 nutritional count per serving 28.1g total fat (17g saturated fat); 1329kJ (318 cal); 6g carbohydrate; 11.2g protein; 3g fibre

Peel 5 of 7 medium zucchini, then coarsely grate all zucchini. Melt 30g butter in large frying pan, add grated zucchini; cook, stirring, about 10 minutes or until softened and excess liquid is evaporated. Meanwhile, melt 30g butter in medium frying pan; cook 2 finely chopped brown onions, stirring, until soft. Combine zucchini, onion and ¼ cup thinly sliced fresh basil in medium bowl. Preheat oven to 200°C/180°C fan-forced. Whisk 3 eggs, ¾ cup crème fraîche or sour cream and ⅓ cup grated gruyère cheese in medium jug. Spread zucchini mixture into 2-litre (8-cup) oiled shallow ovenproof dish. Top with the egg mixture, swirl with a knife to mix lightly. Sprinkle with ½ cup coarsely grated gruyère cheese. Bake about 25 minutes or until browned lightly.

PUMPKIN GRATIN

prep & cook time 1 hour serves 4 nutritional count per serving 9.5g total fat (6.1g saturated fat); 660kJ (158 cal); 11.2g carbohydrate; 6g protein; 2.3g fibre

Preheat oven to 200°C/180°C fan-forced. Peel 750g butternut pumpkin, remove seeds; chop pumpkin into even-sized pieces. Place pumpkin and 2 peeled and halved garlic cloves in oiled small ovenproof dish. Bake about 25 minutes or until pumpkin is almost cooked through. Pour ¼ cup cream over pumpkin in dish; sprinkle with ⅓ cup grated parmesan cheese. Bake another 25 minutes or until pumpkin is tender and top is browned lightly.

VEGIE GRATINS

CAULIFLOWER GRATIN

prep & cook time **30 minutes** serves **6** nutritional count per serving **14.1g total fat (9g saturated fat); 865kJ (207 cal); 10.2g carbohydrate; 9.1g protein; 2.2g fibre**

Preheat oven to 220°C/200°C fan-forced. Boil, steam or microwave 6 trimmed baby cauliflowers until tender; drain. Place in medium shallow ovenproof dish. Meanwhile, melt 50g butter in medium saucepan, add ¼ cup plain flour; cook, stirring, until mixture bubbles and thickens. Gradually stir in 1½ cups hot milk until smooth; cook, stirring, until mixture boils and thickens. Remove from heat, stir in ½ cup grated cheddar cheese and ¼ cup grated parmesan cheese. Pour cheese sauce over cauliflowers; sprinkle with 1 tablespoon packaged breadcrumbs. Bake in oven about 15 minutes or until browned lightly.

note **Use a whole cauliflower, cut into florets, if you can't find baby cauliflower.**

PUMPKIN, FENNEL AND GORGONZOLA GRATIN

prep & cook time **35 minutes** serves **4** nutritional count per serving **65.2g total fat (42.8g saturated fat); 3064kJ (733 cal); 22.9g carbohydrate; 14g protein; 3.5g fibre**

Preheat oven to 200°C/180°C fan-forced. Oil four 1-cup (250ml) shallow ovenproof dishes. Boil, steam or microwave 800g thinly sliced pumpkin until tender. Slice 2 baby fennel bulbs and fronds thinly. Layer fennel, half the fronds, pumpkin and 75g crumbled gorgonzola cheese in dishes. Blend 1 tablespoon plain flour with 2 tablespoons cream in small saucepan; stir in 1¾ cups cream. Stir over heat until mixture boils and thickens. Pour cream mixture into dishes. Cover dishes with foil; bake, in oven, 20 minutes. Preheat grill. Remove foil from dishes; sprinkle dishes with ½ cup stale breadcrumbs and 50g crumbled gorgonzola cheese. Cook under grill until browned. Serve gratins sprinkled with remaining fennel fronds.

POTATO AND THYME GRATIN

prep & cook time **45 minutes** serves **4** nutritional count
per serving **29.1g total fat (16.5g saturated fat); 2128kJ
(509 cal); 42.8g carbohydrate; 17.1g protein; 4.8g fibre**

Preheat oven to 220°C/200°C fan-forced. Oil
four 1-cup (250ml) shallow ovenproof dishes.
Melt 10g butter in medium pan; cook 1 thinly
sliced onion, stirring, until softened. Remove
from pan. Melt 40g butter in same pan; cook
2 tablespoons plain flour, stirring, until mixture
thickens. Gradually stir in 1 cup milk; cook,
stirring, until sauce boils and thickens. Remove
from heat; stir in 2 teaspoons finely chopped
fresh thyme and ½ cup grated cheddar cheese.
Use potato masher to gently crush 600g halved
leftover roast potatoes in large bowl; stir in onion
mixture. Stir white sauce into potato mixture.
Spoon gratin mixture into dishes; sprinkle each
with ½ cup grated cheddar cheese. Bake, in
oven, about 20 minutes or until browned lightly.

POTATO AND ANCHOVY GRATIN

prep & cook time **55 minutes** serves **6** nutritional count
per serving **22.9g total fat (14.9g saturated fat); 1241kJ
(297 cal); 16.1g carbohydrate; 6.3g protein; 1.8g fibre**

Preheat oven to 200°C/180°C fan-forced. Oil
six-hole (¾-cup/180ml) texas muffin pan; line
each hole with two criss-crossed 5cm x 20cm
strips of baking paper. Using sharp knife, V-slicer
or mandoline, cut 700g potatoes and 1 small
onion into very thin slices. Drain and reserve
oil from 12 anchovy fillets in oil (you need
2 teaspoons oil); chop anchovies coarsely.
Layer potato, onion and anchovy in pan holes,
starting and finishing with potato. Heat reserved
anchovy oil, 300ml cream and ½ cup milk in
small saucepan. Pour hot cream mixture over
potato mixture. Bake, in oven, 35 minutes or
until potato is tender. Stand in pan 10 minutes.
Using baking-paper strips as lifters, remove
gratin from pan holes. Serve gratin sprinkled
with 2 tablespoons finely chopped fresh dill.

POTATO GRATINS

POTATO CAULIFLOWER GRATIN

prep & cook time **1¼ hours** serves **6** nutritional count
per serving **7.9g total fat (4.1g saturated fat); 1237kJ
(296 cal); 36.3g carbohydrate; 15.9g protein; 7.4g fibre**

Preheat oven to 200°C/180°C fan-forced. Boil,
steam or microwave 4 finely chopped carrots
until very tender; drain. Blend or process carrot,
2 eggs, ½ cup skim milk and ½ cup light sour
cream until smooth. Meanwhile, boil, steam or
microwave 800g chopped potatoes and 400g
chopped cauliflower, separately, until tender;
drain. Combine potato, cauliflower and 4 finely
chopped green onions in 2-litre (8-cup) ovenproof
dish; pour carrot mixture over potato mixture.
Combine 1½ cups stale breadcrumbs, 2 crushed
garlic cloves and ⅔ cup grated cheddar cheese
in small bowl; sprinkle over carrot mixture. Bake,
in oven, 40 minutes or until browned lightly.

FENNEL AND POTATO GRATIN

prep & cook time **1½ hours** serves **8** nutritional count
per serving **15.2g total fat (9.9g saturated fat); 803kJ
(192 cal); 9.8g carbohydrate; 3.8g protein; 1.3g fibre**

Preheat oven to 180°C/160°C fan-forced. Oil
2-litre (8-cup) ovenproof dish. Using sharp
knife, mandoline or V-slicer, cut 800g potatoes
into very thin slices; pat dry with absorbent
paper. Thinly slice 2 small fennel bulbs. Layer a
quarter of the potato into dish; top with a third
of the fennel. Continue layering potato and
fennel, finishing with potato. Blend 1 tablespoon
plain flour with 2 tablespoons cream in medium
jug to form a smooth paste; stir in 1⅔ cups
cream and ¼ cup milk. Pour cream mixture
over potato; dot with 20g butter. Cover dish
with foil; bake about 1 hour or until vegetables
are tender. Remove foil, top with combined
¾ cup grated cheddar cheese and ¾ cup stale
breadcrumbs; bake about 15 minutes or until
top is browned lightly.

SHEPHERD'S PIE

prep & cook time 1 hour **serves** 4 **nutritional count
per serving** 36.2g total fat (20.2g saturated fat); 2976kJ
(712 cal); 44.7g carbohydrate; 48.8g protein; 6g fibre

30g butter
1 medium brown onion (150g), chopped finely
1 medium carrot (120g), chopped finely
½ teaspoon dried mixed herbs
4 cups (750g) finely chopped cooked lamb
¼ cup (70g) tomato paste
¼ cup (60ml) tomato sauce
2 tablespoons worcestershire sauce
2 cups (500ml) beef stock
2 tablespoons plain flour
⅓ cup (80ml) water
potato topping
5 medium potatoes (1kg), chopped coarsely
60g butter
¼ cup (60ml) milk

1 Preheat oven to 200°C/180°C fan-forced.
Oil shallow 2.5-litre (10-cup) ovenproof dish.
2 Make potato topping.
3 Meanwhile, heat butter in large saucepan;
cook onion and carrot, stirring, until tender.
Add mixed herbs and lamb; cook, stirring,
2 minutes. Stir in paste, sauces and stock,
then blended flour and water; stir over heat
until mixture boils and thickens. Season to
taste. Pour mixture into dish.
4 Drop heaped tablespoons of potato topping
on top of lamb mixture. Bake in oven about
20 minutes or until heated through.
potato topping Boil, steam or microwave
potato until tender; drain. Mash with butter
and milk until smooth.

BAKES

BEEF AND EGGPLANT BAKE WITH POLENTA CRUST

prep & cook time 1¾ hours serves 6 nutritional count
per serving 19.9g total fat (8.7g saturated fat); 1877kJ
(449 cal); 32g carbohydrates; 32.3g protein; 4.7g fibre

1 tablespoon olive oil
1 medium brown onion (150g),
   chopped finely
1 clove garlic, crushed
1 medium red capsicum (200g),
   chopped coarsely
500g beef mince
2 tablespoons tomato paste
½ cup (125ml) dry red wine
400g can whole tomatoes
1 cup firmly packed fresh basil leaves
1 tablespoon fresh oregano leaves
2 medium eggplants (600g), sliced thickly
2 cups (500ml) chicken stock
2 cups (500ml) milk
1 cup (170g) polenta
1½ cups (150g) grated mozzarella cheese

1 Heat oil in large frying pan; cook onion, garlic
and capsicum, stirring, until onion softens. Add
beef; cook, stirring, until beef changes colour.
Add paste; cook, stirring, 2 minutes. Add wine;
cook, stirring, 5 minutes. Add undrained
tomatoes; bring to the boil. Simmer, uncovered,
stirring occasionally, about 15 minutes or until
liquid is almost evaporated. Chop about a
quarter of the basil leaves coarsely; stir into
sauce with oregano.
2 Preheat oven to 200°C/180°C fan-forced.
3 Cook eggplant on heated oiled grill plate
(or grill or barbecue) until browned lightly.
4 Combine stock and milk in medium pan;
bring to the boil. Gradually add polenta, stirring
constantly. Reduce heat; simmer, stirring, about
10 minutes or until polenta thickens.
5 Arrange half the eggplant in shallow 3-litre
(12-cup) baking dish; top with half the beef
mixture. Top with remaining eggplant then
remaining beef mixture and remaining basil.
Spread polenta over basil; sprinkle over cheese.
Bake, in oven, 20 minutes or until top is browned
lightly. Stand 10 minutes before serving.

note Have you ever eaten eggplant that's bitter? It's
easy to avoid this taste by simply treating the eggplant
to a process known as disgorging. Cut the eggplant,
place in a colander, sprinkle all over with salt then stand
for at least half an hour. The salt will turn slightly brown
as it absorbs the bitter liquid. Rinse eggplant pieces
under cold water then pat dry with absorbent paper.

spinach and herb cannelloni

SPINACH AND HERB CANNELLONI

prep & cook time **1 hour** serves **6** nutritional count
per serving **31g** total fat (17.1g saturated fat); 2412kJ
(577 cal); 41.8g carbohydrate; 28.7g protein; 8.3g fibre

1kg spinach, trimmed, chopped coarsely
500g ricotta cheese
2 eggs
1½ cups (120g) grated parmesan cheese
¼ cup finely chopped fresh mint
3 teaspoons finely chopped fresh thyme
2 teaspoons finely chopped fresh rosemary
250g cannelloni tubes
creamy tomato sauce
1 tablespoon olive oil
1 medium brown onion (150g), chopped finely
4 cloves garlic, crushed
4 x 400g cans diced tomatoes
½ cup (125ml) cream
1 teaspoon white sugar

1 Make creamy tomato sauce.
2 Preheat oven to 180°C/160°C fan-forced.
3 Cook washed spinach in heated large pan,
stirring, until wilted. Drain; when cool enough
to handle, squeeze out excess moisture.
4 Combine spinach in large bowl with ricotta,
eggs, ½ cup of the parmesan and herbs. Using
large piping bag, fill pasta with spinach mixture.
5 Spread a third of the creamy tomato sauce
into shallow 25cm x 35cm ovenproof dish; top
with pasta, in a single layer, then with remaining
sauce. Bake cannelloni, covered, in oven,
20 minutes. Uncover, sprinkle cannelloni with
remaining parmesan; bake about 15 minutes or
until pasta is tender and cheese is browned lightly.
creamy tomato sauce Heat oil in large pan;
cook onion, stirring, until softened. Add garlic;
stir until fragrant. Add undrained tomatoes; bring
to the boil. Reduce heat; simmer, uncovered,
stirring occasionally, about 20 minutes or until
sauce thickens slightly. Cool 10 minutes; blend
or process sauce with cream and sugar until
smooth. Season to taste.

MACARONI CHEESE WITH OLIVES

prep & cook time **35 minutes** serves **4** nutritional count
per serving **29.5g** total fat (18.4g saturated fat); 3223kJ
(771 cal); 90.1g carbohydrate; 32.4g protein; 6.7g fibre

375g elbow macaroni pasta
60g butter
1 small red onion (100g), sliced thinly
1 clove garlic, crushed
1 medium red capsicum (200g), sliced thinly
150g button mushrooms, sliced thinly
⅓ cup (50g) plain flour
3 cups (750ml) milk
⅓ cup (95g) tomato paste
⅓ cup (40g) seeded black olives, halved
½ cup finely chopped fresh basil
1½ cups (150g) pizza cheese

1 Cook pasta in large saucepan of boiling water
until just tender; drain.
2 Melt butter in large pan; cook onion, garlic,
capsicum and mushrooms, stirring, until soft.
Add flour; cook, stirring, until mixture bubbles
and thickens. Gradually stir in milk. Add paste;
cook, stirring, until sauce boils and thickens.
3 Preheat grill.
4 Stir pasta, olives, basil and half the cheese
into sauce. Place mixture in deep 2-litre (8-cup)
ovenproof dish; sprinkle with remaining cheese.
Grill until cheese melts and is browned lightly.

macaroni cheese with olives

CHICKEN ENCHILADAS

prep & cook time 1½ hours serves 10 nutritional count
per serving 9.4g total fat (9.4g saturated fat); 1593kJ
(381 cal); 29.4g carbohydrate; 22g protein; 3.1g fibre

3 chipotle chillies
1 cup (250ml) boiling water
500g chicken breast fillets
1 tablespoon vegetable oil
1 large red onion (300g), chopped finely
2 cloves garlic, crushed
1 teaspoon ground cumin
1 tablespoon tomato paste
2 x 425g cans crushed tomatoes
1 tablespoon finely chopped fresh oregano
⅔ cup (160g) sour cream
1½ cups (240g) grated cheddar cheese
10 small flour tortillas

1 Cover chillies with the water in small
heatproof bowl; stand 20 minutes. Remove
and discard stems from chillies; blend chillies
with the soaking liquid until smooth.
2 Meanwhile, place chicken in medium pan of
boiling water; return to the boil. Reduce heat;
simmer, covered, about 10 minutes or until
chicken is cooked through. Remove chicken
from poaching liquid; cool 10 minutes. Discard
poaching liquid; shred chicken finely.

3 Preheat oven to 180°C/160°C fan-forced.
Oil shallow rectangular 3-litre (12-cup)
ovenproof dish.
4 Heat oil in large frying pan; cook onion,
stirring, until soft. Reserve half the onion
mixture in small bowl.
5 Add garlic and cumin to remaining onion in
pan; cook, stirring, until fragrant. Add chilli
mixture, tomato paste, undrained tomatoes
and oregano; bring to the boil. Reduce heat;
simmer, uncovered, 1 minute. Remove sauce
from heat; season to taste.
6 Meanwhile, combine shredded chicken,
reserved onion, half the sour cream and a
third of the cheese in medium bowl.
7 Warm tortillas according to instructions on
packet. Dip tortillas, one at a time, in tomato
sauce in pan; place on board. Place ¼ cup of
the chicken mixture along edge of each tortilla;
roll enchiladas to enclose filling.
8 Spread ½ cup tomato sauce into prepared
dish. Place enchiladas, seam-side down, in dish
(they should fit snugly, without overcrowding).
Pour remaining tomato sauce over enchiladas;
sprinkle with remaining cheese. Bake, in oven,
about 15 minutes or until cheese melts and
enchiladas are heated through. Sprinkle
enchiladas with fresh coriander leaves, if you
like, and serve with remaining sour cream.

note Chipotle is the name given to the fresh jalapeño
chilli after it's been dried and smoked. Having a deep,
intensely smoky flavour rather than a searing heat,
chipotles are dark brown, almost black, in colour and
wrinkled in appearance. They are available from
specialty spice stores and gourmet delicatessens.

blue cheese penne bake

BAKED KUMARA GNOCCHI WITH GARLIC CREAM SAUCE

prep & cook time **1¾ hours (+ cooling)** serves **6**
nutritional count per serving **57.6g total fat**
(32g saturated fat); 3474kJ (831 cal);
59.4g carbohydrate; 17.2g protein; 5.9g fibre

2 large kumara (1kg), chopped coarsely
4 small potatoes (480g), chopped coarsely
1½ cups (225g) plain flour
1 teaspoon ground nutmeg
½ cup (80g) roasted pine nuts
1 cup (80g) grated parmesan cheese
garlic cream sauce
600ml cream
2 cloves garlic, crushed

1 Preheat oven to 180°C/160°C fan-forced.
2 Roast kumara and potato, in single layer, on oiled oven tray about 1 hour or until vegetables are tender; cool.
3 Meanwhile, make garlic cream sauce.
4 Increase oven to 200°C/180°C fan-forced. Oil 6 x 2-cup (500ml) ovenproof dishes.
5 Mash kumara and potato in large bowl until smooth; add sifted flour and nutmeg, stir to a soft, sticky dough.
6 Divide dough into quarters; flatten quarters on floured surface to 1cm thickness. Cut 5cm rounds from dough; transfer gnocchi to tray lined with tea towel. Reshape and cut rounds from remaining dough until all dough is used.
7 Cook gnocchi, in batches, in large pan of boiling water, about 3 minutes or until gnocchi float to the surface. Using slotted spoon, remove gnocchi from pan. Divide gnocchi among dishes, top with garlic cream sauce, pine nuts and cheese. Bake, in oven, about 15 minutes or until golden brown. To serve, top with a little extra finely grated parmesan cheese.
garlic cream sauce Combine cream and garlic in medium pan; bring to the boil. Reduce heat; simmer, uncovered, about 5 minutes or until thickened slightly. Season to taste.

BLUE CHEESE PENNE BAKE

prep & cook time **55 minutes** serves **4** nutritional count per serving **27.4g total fat (14.8g saturated fat); 2433kJ (582 cal); 54.2g carbohydrate; 27.1g protein; 4.9g fibre**

6 small egg tomatoes (360g), halved
1 tablespoon olive oil
1 teaspoon sea salt
1 teaspoon freshly ground black pepper
300g penne pasta
125g blue cheese, crumbled
125g light cream cheese, softened
200g baby spinach leaves
1 cup (80g) grated parmesan cheese

1 Drizzle tomato with oil, salt and pepper; cook, cut-side down, on heated oiled grill plate (or grill or barbecue) 10 minutes or until soft and browned lightly; keep warm.
2 Cook pasta in large saucepan of boiling water until just tender; drain. Return pasta to pan with blue cheese, cream cheese, spinach and half the parmesan; toss gently until well combined.
3 Preheat grill to hot. Place pasta mixture in oiled shallow 2.5-litre (10 cup) ovenproof dish, sprinkle with remaining parmesan; cook under grill until top is browned lightly. Serve bake with tomatoes.

baked kumara gnocchi with garlic cream sauce

moussaka

MOUSSAKA

prep & cook time **1¾ hours** serves **6** nutritional count
per serving 36.6g total fat (16.5g saturated fat); 2420kJ
(579 cal); 18g carbohydrate; 41.8g protein; 5.3g fibre

¼ cup (60ml) olive oil
2 large eggplants (1kg), sliced thinly
1 large brown onion (200g), chopped finely
2 cloves garlic, crushed
1kg lamb mince
425g can crushed tomatoes
½ cup (125ml) dry white wine
1 teaspoon ground cinnamon
¼ cup (20g) grated parmesan cheese
white sauce
80g butter
⅓ cup (50g) plain flour
2 cups (500ml) milk

1 Heat oil in large frying pan; cook eggplant, in
batches, until browned; drain on absorbent paper.
2 Cook onion and garlic in pan until soft. Add
mince; cook, stirring, until mince changes colour.
Stir in undrained tomatoes, wine and cinnamon;
bring to the boil. Simmer, uncovered, about
30 minutes or until liquid has evaporated.
3 Preheat oven to 180°C/160°C fan-forced. Oil
shallow 2-litre (8-cup) rectangular baking dish.
4 Make white sauce.
5 Place a third of the eggplant, overlapping
slightly, in dish; spread half the meat sauce
over eggplant. Repeat with another third of the
eggplant, remaining meat sauce then remaining
eggplant. Spread white sauce over eggplant;
sprinkle with cheese.
6 Bake about 40 minutes or until top browns
lightly. Cover; stand 10 minutes before serving.
white sauce Melt butter in medium pan. Add
flour; cook, stirring, until mixture bubbles and
thickens. Gradually add milk; stir until mixture
boils and thickens.

CHICKEN AND LEEK LASAGNE

prep & cook time **1½ hours** serves **4** nutritional count
per serving 24.8g total fat (8.5g saturated fat); 1685kJ
(403 cal); 15.5g carbohydrate; 28.8g protein; 2.4g fibre

60g butter
1 large leek (500g), sliced thinly

chicken and leek lasagne

¼ cup (35g) plain flour
2 teaspoons dijon mustard
2 cups (500ml) chicken stock, warmed
3 cups (480g) shredded barbecued chicken
4 fresh lasagne sheets (200g), trimmed to fit
baking dish
⅔ cup (80g) grated cheddar cheese

1 Preheat oven to 180°C/160°C fan-forced.
2 Melt butter in medium pan; cook leek, stirring,
until soft. Add flour; cook, stirring, until mixture
thickens and bubbles. Gradually stir in mustard
and stock over medium heat until mixture boils
and thickens. Reserve ⅔ cup of the white sauce;
stir chicken into remaining sauce.
3 Oil shallow 2-litre (8-cup) ovenproof dish.
Cover base with lasagne sheet; top with about
a quarter of the warm chicken mixture. Repeat
layering with remaining lasagne sheets and
chicken mixture, finishing with chicken mixture;
top with reserved white sauce and the cheese.
4 Bake, covered, in oven, 30 minutes; uncover,
bake a further 20 minutes or until browned lightly.
Stand 5 minutes before serving.

note **You need to buy a large barbecued chicken
weighing about 900g for this recipe.**

cottage pie

COTTAGE PIE

prep & cook time **2 hours** serves **8** nutritional count
per serving **16.5g total fat (7.6g saturated fat); 1659kJ
(397 cal); 23.9g carbohydrate; 35.2g protein; 6g fibre**

1 tablespoon olive oil
2 cloves garlic, crushed
1 large brown onion (200g), chopped finely
2 medium carrots (240g), chopped finely
1kg beef mince
1 tablespoon worcestershire sauce
2 tablespoons tomato paste
2 x 425g cans crushed tomatoes
1 teaspoon dried mixed herbs
200g button mushrooms, quartered
1 cup (120g) frozen peas
1kg potatoes, chopped coarsely
¾ cup (180ml) hot milk
40g butter, softened
½ cup (50g) pizza cheese

1 Heat oil in large saucepan; cook garlic, onion
and carrot, stirring, until onion softens. Add
mince; cook, stirring, about 10 minutes or until
changed in colour.
2 Add sauce, paste, undrained tomatoes and
herbs; bring to the boil. Reduce heat; simmer,

uncovered, about 30 minutes or until mixture
thickens slightly. Stir in mushrooms and peas;
season to taste.
3 Meanwhile, preheat oven to 180°C/160°C
fan-forced.
4 Boil, steam or microwave potato until tender;
drain. Mash potato with milk and butter.
5 Pour mince mixture into deep 3-litre (12-cup)
ovenproof dish; top with potato mixture,
sprinkle with cheese. Bake, in oven, about
45 minutes or until pie is heated through and
top is browned lightly.

PEA AND SALMON PASTA BAKE

prep & cook time **50 minutes** serves **6** nutritional count
per serving **23.8g total fat (13.7g saturated fat); 2345kJ
(561 cal); 51.2g carbohydrate; 33.1g protein; 3.9g fibre**

375g rigatoni pasta
40g butter
2 tablespoons plain flour
2 cups (500ml) milk
1½ cups (180g) frozen peas
½ cup (40g) grated parmesan cheese
1¼ cups (150g) grated cheddar cheese
415g can pink salmon, drained, skin and
    bones removed

1 Preheat oven to 200°C/180°C fan-forced.
2 Cook pasta in large saucepan of boiling water
until tender; drain.
3 Meanwhile, melt butter in medium saucepan.
Add flour; cook, stirring, until mixture thickens
and bubbles. Gradually stir in milk over medium
heat until sauce boils and thickens. Stir in peas,
¼ cup parmesan and ¾ cup cheddar cheese.
4 Combine sauce mixture, pasta and salmon in
oiled shallow 2.5-litre (10-cup) ovenproof dish;
sprinkle with remaining combined cheeses.
Bake, in oven, about 20 minutes or until
browned lightly.

pea and salmon pasta bake

ITALIAN SAUSAGE AND THREE-CHEESE LASAGNE

prep & cook time 2¾ hours serves 8 nutritional count
per serving 46.8g total fat (23.1g saturated fat); 3227kJ
(772 cal); 44g carbohydrate; 39.3g protein; 5.4g fibre

500g italian sausages
250g frozen chopped spinach, thawed,
  drained
250g ricotta cheese
½ cup (40g) grated parmesan cheese
¼ teaspoon ground nutmeg
1 egg
6 sheets fresh lasagne
250g mozzarella cheese, sliced thinly
tomato sauce
1 tablespoon olive oil
1 medium onion (150g), chopped finely
1 medium carrot (120g), chopped finely
1 trimmed celery stalk (100g), chopped finely
5 x 8cm long parsley stalks, crushed
2 cloves garlic, crushed
½ cup (125ml) dry red wine
¼ cup (70g) tomato paste
2⅔ cups (700g) bottled tomato pasta sauce
cheese sauce
50g butter
⅓ cup (50g) plain flour
2 cups (500ml) milk
1½ cups (120g) grated parmesan cheese

1 Make tomato sauce. Make cheese sauce.
2 Preheat oven to 200°C/180°C fan-forced.
3 Cook sausages in oiled large frying pan until browned all over; drain then slice thinly.
4 Combine spinach, ricotta, parmesan, nutmeg and egg in medium bowl.
5 Spread ½ cup of the cheese sauce over base of 20cm x 30cm ovenproof dish. Top with two pasta sheets (trim to fit dish) then spread with half the spinach mixture. Sprinkle with half the sausage; cover with 1 cup of the tomato sauce then half the remaining cheese sauce.
6 Top with two pasta sheets. Spread remaining spinach mixture over pasta; sprinkle with remaining sausage. Spread with 1 cup tomato sauce, then remaining cheese sauce. Top with remaining pasta, then half the remaining tomato sauce. Top with mozzarella then spread with remaining tomato sauce.
7 Bake lasagne, covered, in oven, 30 minutes. Uncover, bake a further 10 minutes or until lasagne is browned lightly. Stand 10 minutes before serving.

tomato sauce Heat oil in large saucepan; cook onion, carrot, celery and parsley, stirring occasionally, until vegetables soften. Add garlic; cook, stirring, 1 minute. Add wine; cook, stirring, until almost evaporated. Discard parsley stalks. Add paste; cook, stirring, 3 minutes. Add pasta sauce; simmer, uncovered, about 15 minutes or until sauce thickens slightly. Season to taste.
cheese sauce Melt butter in medium saucepan, add flour; cook, stirring, until mixture thickens and bubbles. Gradually stir in milk until mixture boils and thickens. Reduce heat; cook, stirring, 1 minute, remove from heat. Add cheese, stir until melted.

four cheese pasta bake

FOUR CHEESE PASTA BAKE

prep & cook time **50 minutes** serves **6** nutritional count
per serving **38.9g total fat (17.5g saturated fat); 3724kJ
(891 cal); 88.2g carbohydrates; 36.4g protein; 7.2g fibre**

500g penne pasta
4 green onions, chopped finely
½ cup (75g) drained semi-dried tomatoes,
  chopped coarsely
2 tablespoons olive oil
2 cloves garlic, crushed
¼ cup coarsely chopped fresh basil
½ loaf turkish bread (220g), cut into 1cm pieces
four-cheese sauce
50g butter
⅓ cup (50g) plain flour
1 litre (4 cups) milk
⅓ cup (35g) grated fontina cheese
¾ cup (75g) grated mozzarella cheese
¾ cup (60g) grated parmesan cheese
100g gorgonzola cheese, crumbled

1 Preheat oven to 180°C/160°C fan-forced. Oil
deep 3-litre (12-cup) ovenproof dish.
2 Cook pasta in large saucepan of boiling water
until tender.
3 Meanwhile, make four-cheese sauce.

4 Drain pasta; return to same pan with onion,
tomato and cheese sauce; toss gently. Season
to taste. Transfer pasta mixture to prepared dish.
5 Combine oil, garlic and basil in medium bowl,
add bread; toss bread mixture gently.
6 Sprinkle bread mixture over pasta bake in
even layer; bake about 15 minutes or until top
is browned lightly and pasta is heated through.
four-cheese sauce Melt butter in medium pan,
add flour; cook, stirring, until mixture bubbles
and thickens. Gradually add milk; cook, stirring,
until sauce boils and thickens. Remove from
heat, add cheeses; stir until smooth.

CHICKEN, MUSHROOM AND ASPARAGUS CREAMY PASTA BAKE

prep & cook time **50 minutes** serves **4** nutritional count
per serving **37.3g total fat (22.3g saturated fat); 3775kJ
(903 cal); 75.2g carbohydrate; 64g protein; 4.8g fibre**

375g rigatoni pasta
60g butter
600g breast fillets, diced into 1cm pieces
100g button mushrooms, sliced thinly
2 tablespoons plain flour
2 cups (500ml) milk
½ cup (40g) grated romano cheese
1¼ cups (150g) grated cheddar cheese
170g asparagus, trimmed, chopped coarsely
¼ cup coarsely chopped fresh flat-leaf parsley

1 Preheat oven to 200°C/180°C fan-forced.
2 Cook pasta in large saucepan of boiling water
until tender; drain.
3 Heat a third of the butter in large frying pan;
cook chicken, in batches, until cooked through.
Remove from pan.
4 Heat remaining butter in same pan; cook
mushrooms, stirring, until tender. Add flour;
cook, stirring, 1 minute. Gradually stir in milk
over medium heat until mixture boils and
thickens. Stir in chicken, ¼ cup of the romano,
¾ cup of the cheddar and the asparagus.
Season to taste.
5 Combine chicken mixture and drained pasta
in 2.5 litre (10-cup) ovenproof dish; sprinkle
with remaining cheeses. Bake in oven about
15 minutes or until top browns lightly. Serve
pasta bake sprinkled with parsley.

chicken, mushroom and asparagus creamy pasta bake

ricotta and spinach stuffed pasta shells

RICOTTA AND SPINACH STUFFED PASTA SHELLS

prep & cook time 1½ hours serves 4 nutritional count per serving 10.2g total fat (5.3g saturated fat); 2378kJ (569 cal); 70.3g carbohydrate; 43.4g protein; 9.1g fibre

32 large pasta shells (280g)
500g spinach
250g low-fat ricotta cheese
500g low-fat cottage cheese
2⅓ cups (600g) bottled tomato pasta sauce
1 cup (250ml) vegetable stock
1 tablespoon finely grated parmesan cheese

1 Cook pasta in large saucepan of boiling water 3 minutes; drain. Cool slightly.
2 Preheat oven to 180°C/160°C fan-forced.
3 Boil, steam or microwave spinach until just wilted; drain. When cool enough to handle, chop spinach finely; squeeze out excess liquid.
4 Combine spinach in large bowl with ricotta and cottage cheese; season. Spoon spinach mixture into pasta shells.
5 Combine sauce and stock in oiled shallow 2-litre (8 cup) ovenproof dish. Place pasta shells in dish; sprinkle with parmesan. Bake, covered, about 1 hour or until pasta is tender.

note Large pasta shells, called conchiglioni in Italian, are available from gourmet delicatessens; you can use 16 cannelloni shells instead.

CHICKEN PIE WITH PARSNIP MASH

prep & cook time 1¼ hours serves 6 nutritional count per serving 31.7g total fat (13.5g saturated fat); 2976kJ (712 cal); 49g carbohydrate; 52.4g protein; 10.6g fibre

2 teaspoons vegetable oil
1 medium brown onion (150g), chopped finely
750g chicken mince
1 medium carrot (120g), chopped finely
2 trimmed celery stalks (200g), chopped finely
¼ cup (35g) plain flour
1 cup (250ml) chicken stock
2 tablespoons worcestershire sauce
155g button mushrooms, quartered
¾ cup (120g) frozen peas

chicken pie with parsnip mash

parsnip mash
2 medium parsnips (500g), chopped coarsely
4 medium potatoes (800g), chopped coarsely
¼ cup (60ml) milk
45g butter
½ cup (40g) grated parmesan cheese

1 Make parsnip mash.
2 Preheat oven to 180°C/160°C fan-forced.
3 Heat oil in large saucepan, add onion and chicken; cook, stirring, until browned. Add carrot and celery; cook, stirring, until soft. Stir in flour then gradually add stock, sauce and mushrooms; cook, stirring, until mixture boils and thickens. Stir in peas; season to taste.
4 Spoon mince mixture into 2.5-litre (10-cup) ovenproof dish; top with parsnip mash. Bake about 30 minutes or until browned lightly and heated through.
parsnip mash Boil, steam or microwave parsnip and potato until tender; drain. Mash potato and parsnip with milk and butter until smooth; stir in cheese, season to taste.

BEEF, SPINACH AND MUSHROOM LASAGNE

prep & cook time **2 hours** serves **8** nutritional count
per serving **26.5g total fat (14.1g saturated fat); 1806kJ
(432 cal); 15.9g carbohydrate; 28.1g protein; 5g fibre**

1 tablespoon olive oil
1 medium brown onion (150g), chopped finely
625g beef mince
½ cup (125ml) dry red wine
2 cups (500ml) beef stock
⅓ cup (95g) tomato paste
400g can crushed tomatoes
1 tablespoon finely chopped fresh oregano
30g butter
315g swiss brown mushrooms, sliced thinly
2 cloves garlic, crushed
625g spinach, trimmed
4 fresh lasagne pasta sheets, trim to fit dish
⅓ cup (25g) grated parmesan cheese
white sauce
45g butter
¼ cup (35g) plain flour
2 cups (500ml) milk
1 cup (120g) grated cheddar cheese

1 Preheat oven to 200°C/180°C fan-forced.
2 Heat oil in large saucepan, add onion; cook, stirring, until soft. Add beef; stir until browned. Stir in wine, stock, paste, undrained tomatoes and oregano; bring to the boil. Reduce heat; simmer, covered, 30 minutes. Uncover; simmer a further 30 minutes or until sauce thickens slightly, season to taste.
3 Meanwhile, make white sauce.
4 Melt butter in large frying pan, add mushrooms and garlic; cook, stirring, until mushrooms soften.
5 Boil, steam or microwave spinach until tender; drain. When cool enough to handle, squeeze excess liquid from spinach; chop coarsely.
6 Oil shallow 2.5-litre (10-cup) ovenproof dish. Cover base with trimmed lasagne sheets; top with a third of the beef mixture, a third of the mushrooms and half the white sauce. Top with lasagne sheets; top with another third of the beef mixture, another third of the mushrooms and the spinach. Top with remaining lasagne sheets, beef mixture, mushrooms and white sauce. Sprinkle with cheese.
7 Bake, covered, in oven, about 40 minutes or until pasta is tender.
8 Preheat grill. Uncover lasagne; grill until browned lightly. Stand 5 minutes before serving.
white sauce Melt butter in medium saucepan; stir in flour until mixture bubbles and thickens. Gradually add milk, stirring, until mixture boils and thickens. Remove from heat; stir in cheese.

vegetable and lentil lasagne

VEGETABLE AND LENTIL LASAGNE

prep & cook time **1 hour** serves **4** nutritional count
per serving **22.1g total fat (8.9g saturated fat); 1898kJ
(454 cal); 34.3g carbohydrate; 26g protein; 10.8g fibre**

1 cup (200g) red lentils
2 tablespoons olive oil
1 small leek (200g), sliced thinly
1 fresh long red chilli, chopped finely
2 cloves garlic, crushed
4 medium tomatoes (600g), chopped coarsely
1 tablespoon tomato paste
4 fresh lasagne sheets, trimmed to fit dishes
50g baby spinach leaves
200g ricotta cheese
100g fetta cheese, crumbled
1 tablespoon finely chopped fresh basil

1 Preheat oven to 200°C/180°C fan-forced.
Oil four 1½-cup (375ml) ovenproof dishes.
2 Cook lentils in large pan of boiling water until
just tender; drain.
3 Meanwhile, heat half the oil in large pan; cook
leek, chilli and garlic, stirring, until leek softens.
Add tomato and paste; cook, stirring, until
liquid is almost absorbed. Remove from heat;
stir in lentils. Season to taste.
4 Spoon 1 tablespoon of the lentil mixture into
each dish; cover with lasagne. Divide half the
remaining lentil mixture among dishes; top with
equal amounts of spinach then ricotta. Cover
ricotta with lasagne; top each with remaining
lentil mixture then sprinkle with fetta.
5 Bake in oven about 20 minutes or until heated
through. Stand 5 minutes; sprinkle each lasagne
with basil and drizzle with remaining oil.

note **Use scissors to trim lasagne sheets to fit the dishes.**

CHICKEN AND SPINACH BAKE

prep & cook time **50 minutes** serves **4** nutritional count
per serving **18.8g total fat (7.7g saturated fat); 2195kJ
(525 cal); 49.7g carbohydrate; 34.9g protein; 6.9g fibre**

1 tablespoon olive oil
1 large brown onion (200g), chopped finely
2 cloves garlic, crushed
10 instant lasagne sheets (200g)

chicken and spinach bake

1½ cups (240g) shredded barbecue chicken
1 cup (100g) pizza cheese
3 cups (750g) bottled tomato pasta sauce
2 cups (500ml) water
50g baby spinach leaves
½ cup (120g) firm ricotta cheese, crumbled

1 Heat oil in large shallow flameproof dish; cook
onion and garlic, stirring, until onion softens.
2 Break lasagne sheets into bite-sized pieces.
Sprinkle pasta pieces, chicken and half the
pizza cheese into the dish.
3 Pour combined pasta sauce and the water
over top of chicken mixture. Simmer, covered,
about 20 minutes or until pasta is tender;
season to taste.
4 Meanwhile, preheat grill.
5 Sprinkle bake with spinach, ricotta and
remaining pizza cheese; grill about 5 minutes or
until cheese melts. Stand, covered, 10 minutes
before serving, sprinkled with extra baby
spinach leves.

note **You need to buy half a large barbecued chicken
(450g) for this recipe.**

tuna spinach mornay pie

TUNA SPINACH MORNAY PIE

prep & cook time **50 minutes** serves **4** nutritional count
per serving 25.8g total fat (12.1g saturated fat); 2040kJ
(488 cal); 29.7g carbohydrate; 31.7g protein; 5.8g fibre

50g butter
1 medium brown onion (150g), sliced thinly
¼ cup (35g) plain flour
2 cups (500ml) milk, warmed
150g baby spinach leaves
425g can tuna in springwater, drained
2 tablespoons lemon juice
potato and celeriac mash
400g potatoes, chopped coarsely
300g celeriac, chopped coarsely
2 tablespoons milk
30g butter
¼ cup (20g) grated parmesan cheese

1 Make potato and celeriac mash.
2 Melt butter in medium pan; cook onion,
stirring, about 5 minutes or until softened. Add
flour; cook, stirring, until mixture thickens and
bubbles. Gradually add milk; stir until mixture
boils and thickens. Remove from heat; stir in
spinach, tuna and juice. Season to taste.
3 Preheat grill.

4 Spoon tuna mixture into shallow flameproof
1.5 litre (6-cup) dish; top with mash. Grill until
top is browned lightly.
potato and celeriac mash Boil, steam or
microwave potato and celeriac, separately, until
tender; drain. Combine potato and celeriac in
large bowl; mash with milk and butter until
smooth. Stir in cheese, season to taste; cover
to keep warm.

THREE-CHEESE VEGETARIAN LASAGNE

prep & cook time **55 minutes** serves **4** nutritional count
per serving 38.4g total fat (17.2g saturated fat); 2876kJ
(688 cal); 49.6g carbohydrate; 31.4g protein; 9.9g fibre

2 cups (500g) bottled tomato pasta sauce
3 fresh lasagne sheets (150g), trim to fit dish
¾ cup (110g) drained semi-dried tomatoes
   in oil, chopped coarsely
100g piece fetta cheese, crumbled
½ cup (120g) firm ricotta cheese, crumbled
1½ cups (180g) grated cheddar cheese
1 cup (150g) drained marinated char-grilled
   eggplant, chopped coarsely
¾ cup (165g) drained char-grilled capsicum
125g baby rocket leaves

1 Preheat oven to 200°C/180°C fan-forced.
Oil deep 2.5-litre (10-cup) ovenproof dish.
2 Spread ½ cup pasta sauce over base of
dish; top with a lasagne sheet and another
½ cup pasta sauce. Top with semi-dried tomato,
¼ cup of each cheese, then another lasagne
sheet. Top with ½ cup pasta sauce, eggplant,
remaining fetta, remaining ricotta and another
¼ cup cheddar. Top with remaining lasagne
sheet, remaining sauce and capsicum; sprinkle
with remaining cheddar.
3 Bake, covered, 30 minutes. Uncover; bake
about 15 minutes or until browned lightly. Stand
5 minutes before cutting; serve with rocket.

three-cheese vegetarian lasagne

EGGPLANT BOLOGNESE BAKE

prep & cook time 1¾ hours serves 4 nutritional count
per serving 19.4g total fat (8.7g saturated fat); 1601kJ
(383 cal); 14.4g carbohydrate; 28.7g protein; 8.7g fibre

2 medium eggplants (600g)
200g baby spinach leaves
150g ricotta cheese
1 egg white
½ cup (50g) grated mozzarella cheese
⅓ cup (25g) grated parmesan cheese
bolognese sauce
2 teaspoons olive oil
1 large brown onion (200g), chopped coarsely
1 small red capsicum (150g), chopped coarsely
1 small green capsicum (150g), chopped
    coarsely
2 cloves garlic, crushed
250g beef mince
1 large egg tomato (90g), chopped coarsely
1 tablespoon tomato paste
½ cup (125ml) dry red wine
400g can crushed tomatoes
2 tablespoons coarsely chopped fresh basil
1 tablespoon coarsely chopped fresh oregano
rocket salad
100g baby rocket leaves
½ cup loosely packed fresh basil leaves
1 tablespoon balsamic vinegar
1 teaspoon olive oil

1 Make bolognese sauce.

2 Meanwhile, cut eggplants into 2mm slices; cook on heated oiled grill plate (or grill or barbecue) until just tender.

3 Preheat oven to 180°C/160°C fan-forced.

4 Boil, steam or microwave spinach until wilted; drain. When cool enough to handle, squeeze excess liquid from spinach. Combine spinach, ricotta and egg white in medium bowl.

5 Spread 1 cup of the sauce over base of shallow 2-litre (8-cup) ovenproof dish. Top with half the eggplant, then half the spinach mixture, another cup of sauce, remaining eggplant and remaining spinach mixture. Spread remaining sauce over the top then sprinkle with combined cheeses. Bake, in oven, about 20 minutes or until top browns lightly. Stand 10 minutes.

6 Meanwhile, make rocket salad. Serve bake with rocket salad.

bolognese sauce Heat oil in medium frying pan; cook onion, capsicums and garlic, stirring, until onion softens. Add beef to pan; cook, stirring, until beef changes colour. Add chopped tomato and tomato paste; cook, stirring, 3 minutes. Stir in wine and undrained tomatoes; bring to the boil. Simmer, uncovered, about 25 minutes or until sauce thickens. Remove from heat; stir in herbs. Season to taste.

rocket salad Combine ingredients in bowl.

pumpkin and goat's cheese lasagne stacks

PUMPKIN AND GOAT'S CHEESE LASAGNE STACKS

prep & cook time 1¼ hours makes 6 nutritional count per stack 14.1g total fat (7.6g saturated fat); 1016kJ (243 cal); 17g carbohydrate; 11.1g protein; 2.3g fibre

700g piece butternut pumpkin, peeled
1 tablespoon olive oil
3 fresh lasagne sheets (150g)
150g baby spinach leaves
120g goat's cheese, chopped finely
¼ cup (20g) grated parmesan cheese
white sauce
20g butter
1 tablespoon plain flour
1½ cups (375ml) milk
¼ cup (20g) grated parmesan cheese

1 Preheat oven to 200°C/180°C fan-forced. Oil six-hole (¾-cup/180ml) texas muffin pan; line pan holes with two criss-crossed 5cm x 20cm strips of baking paper.
2 Cut pumpkin lengthways into 1cm-thick slices. Cut 6 x 7cm rounds and 6 x 8cm rounds from pumpkin. Brush rounds with oil; place in large baking dish in a single layer. Roast about 15 minutes or until tender.
3 Meanwhile, cut 6 x 7cm rounds and 12 x 8cm rounds from lasagne sheets.
4 Make white sauce.
5 Cook spinach until wilted; drain. Refresh in cold water; drain. Squeeze out excess moisture then chop coarsely; spread on absorbent paper.
6 Divide a third of the white sauce among pan holes; place one small pasta round in each hole; top with half the goat's cheese, half the spinach then a small pumpkin round. Repeat layers with another third of the sauce, six large pasta rounds, remaining goat's cheese, spinach and pumpkin. Top lasagne stacks with remaining pasta rounds then white sauce; sprinkle with parmesan.
7 Bake about 25 minutes or until browned lightly. Stand 5 minutes then using baking paper strips as lifters, carefully remove lasagne from pan holes.
white sauce Melt butter in medium pan, add flour; cook, stirring, 1 minute. Gradually stir in milk until sauce boils and thickens. Stir in cheese.

POTATO AND TUNA BAKE

prep & cook time 40 minutes serves 4 nutritional count per serving 38.8g total fat (15.9g saturated fat); 2696kJ (645 cal); 28.6g carbohydrate; 41.5g protein; 8.8g fibre

3 medium potatoes (600g), cut into 1cm cubes
20g butter
1 tablespoon olive oil
3 shallots (75g), chopped coarsely
425g can tuna in oil, drained
250g frozen spinach, thawed, drained
½ cup (125ml) milk
1½ cups (180g) grated cheddar cheese
½ cup drained semi-dried tomatoes, chopped coarsely

1 Preheat oven to 220°C/200°C fan-forced. Oil four 1-cup (250ml) shallow baking dishes.
2 Cook potato until almost tender; drain.
3 Heat butter and oil in large frying pan; add potato, cook, stirring, about 10 minutes or until browned lightly. Add shallot; cook until softens. Transfer mixture to medium bowl; coarsely crush potato mixture with fork.
4 Stir tuna, spinach, milk, ½ cup of the cheese and the tomatoes into potato mixture. Divide mixture among dishes; sprinkle with remaining cheese. Bake about 10 minutes or until browned.

potato and tuna bake

penne with kumara and spinach

PENNE WITH KUMARA AND SPINACH

prep & cook time 1¼ hours serves 6 nutritional count per serving 25.3g total fat (9.8g saturated fat); 2450kJ (586 cal); 63.4g carbohydrate; 21.9g protein; 8.4g fibre

2 medium red onions (340g), cut into wedges
2 small kumara (600g), sliced thickly
2 tablespoons olive oil
375g penne pasta
250g frozen spinach, thawed, drained
1½ cups (360g) ricotta cheese
1 clove garlic, crushed
¼ cup (60ml) cream
2 x 400g cans crushed tomatoes
¼ cup (40g) pine nuts
½ cup (40g) grated parmesan cheese

1 Preheat oven to 220°C/200°C fan-forced.
2 Combine onion and kumara with oil in large baking dish; roast, uncovered, stirring once, about 40 minutes or until tender.
3 Meanwhile, cook pasta in large saucepan of boiling water until tender; drain.
4 Combine pasta in large bowl with spinach, ricotta, garlic, cream and tomatoes.
5 Spread kumara mixture over base of 3-litre (12-cup) baking dish. Top with pasta mixture; sprinkle with nuts and parmesan. Bake, covered, 10 minutes. Uncover; bake about 5 minutes or until browned lightly.

SPICY LAMB SAUSAGE PASTA BAKE

prep & cook time 50 minutes serves 6 nutrition count per serving 36.3g total fat (16.5g saturated fat); 3453kJ (826 cal); 67.7g carbohydrate; 57.6g protein; 7.5g fibre

375g tortiglioni pasta
6 spicy lamb sausages (900g)
1 medium brown onion (150g),
    chopped coarsely
1 small eggplant (230g), chopped coarsely
2 medium red capsicums (400g),
    chopped coarsely
3 small green zucchini (270g),
    chopped coarsely
2⅔ cups (700g) bottled tomato pasta sauce
½ cup coarsely chopped fresh basil
2 cups (200g) pizza cheese

spicy lamb sausage pasta bake

1 Preheat oven to 180°C/160°C fan-forced.
2 Cook pasta in large saucepan of boiling water until tender; drain.
3 Meanwhile, cook sausages in heated large frying pan until cooked through; drain on absorbent paper.
4 Cook onion, eggplant, capsicum and zucchini in same pan, stirring, until tender.
5 Cut sausages into 2cm slices; add to vegetables in pan with sauce and basil, stir to combine. Season to taste.
6 Combine pasta and sausage mixture in deep 3-litre (12-cup) casserole dish; sprinkle with cheese. Bake, in oven, about 20 minutes or until browned lightly.

note Tortiglioni, a tubular pasta with a slight curve and grooves on the exterior, works well when baked with a chunky sauce. You can substitute it with rigatoni.

VEGETARIAN LASAGNE

prep & cook time 2¼ hours serves 8 nutritional count per serving 24.2g total fat (12.3g saturated fat); 1960kJ (469 cal); 40g carbohydrate, 23.4g protein, 7.7g fibre

2 tablespoons olive oil
3 fresh basil leaves
2 cloves garlic, crushed
2 x 800g cans crushed tomatoes
2 large red capsicums (700g)
2 large yellow capsicums (700g)
8 baby eggplants (480g), sliced thinly
  lengthways
cooking-oil spray
300g baby spinach leaves
½ cup coarsely chopped fresh basil
500g ricotta cheese
250g packet fresh lasagne sheets
1 cup (100g) grated mozzarella cheese
½ cup (40g) grated parmesan cheese
white sauce
40g butter
2 tablespoons plain flour
1¼ cups (310ml) milk
¼ cup (20g) grated parmesan cheese

1 Heat oil in medium pan; cook basil leaves and garlic, stirring, until fragrant. Add undrained tomatoes; bring to the boil. Simmer, stirring occasionally, about 30 minutes or until sauce thickens. Season to taste.

2 Preheat oven to 240°C/220°C fan-forced.

3 Quarter capsicums; discard seeds and membranes. Roast in oven, skin-side up, until skin blisters and blackens. Cover capsicum pieces with plastic or paper for 5 minutes then peel away skin.

4 Place eggplant, in single layer, on oiled oven trays; spray with oil. Roast about 5 minutes or until just tender. Reduce oven temperature to 200°C/180°C fan-forced.

5 Meanwhile, boil, steam or microwave spinach until just wilted; drain. When cool enough to handle, squeeze excess liquid from spinach. Combine in medium bowl with chopped basil and ricotta.

6 Make white sauce.

7 Place a third of the lasagne sheets in shallow 2.5-litre (10-cup) ovenproof baking dish (trim to fit dish); top with a third of the tomato sauce, a third of the capsicum and a third of the eggplant. Top with another third of the lasagne sheets, a third of the tomato sauce and all of the ricotta mixture. Top with remaining lasagne sheets, tomato sauce, capsicum, eggplant and all of the white sauce; sprinkle with combined mozzarella and parmesan.

8 Place dish on oven tray; bake in oven about 20 minutes or until top browns lightly. Stand lasagne 10 minutes before serving.

white sauce Melt butter in medium pan, add flour; cook, stirring, 1 minute. Gradually stir in milk until mixture boils and thickens. Remove from heat; stir in cheese.

fish mornay

FISH MORNAY

prep & cook time **1 hour** serves **4** nutritional count per serving **46.8g total fat (28.7g saturated fat); 3168kJ (758 cal); 30.2g carbohydrate; 51.2g protein; 6.9g fibre**

2½ cups (625ml) milk
½ small brown onion (40g)
1 bay leaf
6 black peppercorns
4 x 170g firm white fish fillets
3 large potatoes (900g), chopped coarsely
600g celeriac, chopped coarsely
1 egg yolk
½ cup (40g) grated parmesan cheese
¾ cup (180ml) cream
60g butter
¼ cup (35g) plain flour
2 tablespoons coarsely chopped fresh
   flat-leaf parsley

1 Place milk, onion, bay leaf and peppercorns in large saucepan; bring to the boil. Add fish, reduce heat; simmer, covered, about 5 minutes or until cooked through.
2 Remove fish from pan; divide fish among four 1½-cup (375ml) ovenproof dishes. Strain milk through sieve into medium jug. Discard solids; reserve milk.
3 Boil, steam or microwave potato and celeriac, separately, until tender; drain. Push potato and celeriac through sieve into large bowl; stir in egg yolk, cheese, ¼ cup of the cream and half the butter until smooth. Cover to keep warm.
4 Melt remaining butter in medium pan, add flour; cook, stirring, about 3 minutes or until mixture bubbles and thickens slightly. Gradually stir in reserved milk and remaining cream; cook, stirring, until mixture boils and thickens. Stir in parsley; season to taste.
5 Preheat grill.
6 Divide mornay mixture among dishes; cover each with potato mixture. Place dishes on oven tray; place under hot grill until browned lightly.

note **We used trevally fillets in this recipe but you can use any white fish fillets you like.**

baked three-cheese pasta

BAKED THREE-CHEESE PASTA

prep & cook time **40 minutes** serves **4** nutritional count per serving **58.9g total fat (37.8g saturated fat); 3929kJ (940 cal); 66.4g carbohydrate; 35.4g protein; 3.3g fibre**

375g macaroni pasta
300ml cream
⅓ cup (80ml) vegetable stock
1¼ cups (125g) grated fontina cheese
⅓ cup (75g) crumbled gorgonzola cheese
1¼ cups (100g) grated parmesan cheese
1 teaspoon dijon mustard
2 tablespoons finely chopped fresh
   flat-leaf parsley
1 tablespoon finely chopped fresh chives

1 Preheat oven to 180°C/160°C fan-forced.
2 Cook pasta in large saucepan of boiling water until tender; drain.
3 Meanwhile, heat cream and stock in medium pan until hot. Remove from heat, add fontina, gorgonzola and half the parmesan; stir until melted. Add mustard and herbs.
4 Combine cream mixture with drained pasta then pour into oiled 2.5 litre (10-cup) ovenproof dish; sprinkle with remaining parmesan.
5 Bake about 20 minutes or until browned.

LASAGNE BOLOGNESE

prep & cook time 4¼ hours serves 8 nutritional count
per serving 53.2g total fat (29.1g saturated fat); 3657kJ
(874 cal); 44.3g carbohydrate; 52g protein; 3.8g fibre

2 teaspoons olive oil
6 slices pancetta (90g), chopped finely
1 large white onion (200g), chopped finely
1 medium carrot (120g), chopped finely
2 trimmed celery stalks (200g), chopped finely
1kg beef mince
150g chicken livers, trimmed, chopped finely
2 cups (500ml) milk
60g butter
2 cups (500ml) beef stock
1 cup (250ml) dry red wine
410g can tomato puree
2 tablespoons tomato paste
¼ cup finely chopped fresh flat-leaf parsley
2 cups (160g) grated parmesan cheese
pasta
1 cup (150g) plain flour
¼ cup (45g) semolina flour
2 eggs
1 tablespoon olive oil
semolina flour, extra, for dusting
white sauce
125g butter
¾ cup (110g) plain flour
1.25 litres (5 cups) hot milk

1 Heat oil in large heavy-based pan; cook
pancetta, stirring, until crisp. Add onion, carrot
and celery; cook, stirring, until vegetables
soften. Add beef and liver; cook, stirring, until
beef changes colour. Stir in milk and butter;
cook, stirring occasionally, until liquid reduces
by half. Add stock, wine, puree and paste; bring
to the boil. Reduce heat; simmer, uncovered,
1½ hours. Remove from heat; stir in parsley.
Season to taste.
2 Meanwhile, make pasta.
3 Preheat oven to 200°C/180°C fan-forced.
Grease deep 26cm x 35cm baking dish.
4 Make white sauce.

5 Spread about ½ cup of the white sauce over
base of dish. Layer two pasta sheets, a quarter
of the meat sauce,
¼ cup of the cheese and about 1 cup of the
remaining white sauce in dish. Repeat layering
process, starting with pasta sheets and ending
with white sauce; you will have four layers in
total. Top lasagne with remaining cheese.
6 Bake lasagne, uncovered, in oven, about
40 minutes or until top is browned lightly. Stand
10 minutes before cutting.
pasta Process flours, eggs and oil until mixture
forms a ball. Transfer dough to floured surface;
knead about 5 minutes or until smooth. Divide
dough into quarters; roll each piece through
pasta machine set on thickest setting. Fold
long sides of dough into the centre, roll through
machine. Repeat rolling several times, adjusting
setting so pasta sheets become thinner with
each roll; dust pasta with extra semolina flour
when necessary. Roll to second thinnest setting
(1mm thick), making sure that pasta is at least
10cm wide. Cut pasta into 35cm lengths. Cook
pasta sheets in large saucepan of boiling water,
in batches, about 1 minute or until pasta rises
to surface. Transfer to bowl of iced water; drain,
pat dry with absorbent paper towel.
white sauce Melt butter in medium saucepan,
add flour; stir until mixture forms a smooth paste.
Gradually stir in milk; cook, stirring, until sauce
boils and thickens.

notes Fresh or dried lasagne sheets can be substituted
for the homemade pasta; follow directions on the packet
for cooking time.
Semolina is made from crushed durum wheat hearts,
ground to a very fine flour. It is available from most
supermarkets and health-food stores.

lentil cottage pie

LENTIL COTTAGE PIE

prep & cook time 1½ hours serves 4 nutritional count
per serving 7.3g total fat (1.5g saturated fat); 1384kJ
(331 cal); 44.8g carbohydrate; 15.4g protein; 11.8g fibre

4 medium potatoes (800g), chopped coarsely
½ cup (125ml) milk, warmed
4 green onions, chopped finely
½ cup (100g) french-style green lentils
1 tablespoon olive oil
1 large brown onion (200g), chopped finely
1 medium red capsicum (200g), chopped
   coarsely
2 medium zucchini (240g), chopped coarsely
1 medium eggplant (300g), chopped coarsely
2 cloves garlic, crushed
410g can crushed tomatoes

1 Boil, steam or microwave potato until tender;
drain. Mash potato in large bowl with milk and
green onion until smooth.
2 Meanwhile, cook lentils in small pan of boiling
water until just tender; drain. Rinse; drain.
3 Preheat oven to 200°C/180°C fan-forced.
4 Heat oil in medium pan; cook brown onion,
capsicum, zucchini, eggplant and garlic, stirring,
until vegetables soften. Add undrained tomatoes
and lentils; bring to the boil. Simmer, uncovered,
about 10 minutes or until mixture thickens.
Season to taste.
5 Spoon mixture into oiled shallow 2.5-litre
(10-cup) baking dish; top with potato mixture.
Bake 30 minutes or until top browns lightly.

CHEESY VEGIE PASTA BAKE

prep & cook time 35 minutes serves 6 nutritional count
per serving 10.9g total fat (5.4g saturated fat); 1952kJ
(467 cal); 62.3g carbohydrate; 25.5g protein; 7.4g fibre

375g penne pasta
300g broccoli, cut into florets
500g cauliflower, cut into florets
2 teaspoons vegetable oil
1 large brown onion (200g), chopped finely
1 teaspoon mustard powder
1 teaspoon sweet paprika
¼ cup (35g) plain flour
1½ cups (375ml) low-fat milk

cheesy vegie pasta bake

420g can tomato soup
400g can diced tomatoes
1½ cups (180g) grated reduced-fat
   cheddar cheese
2 tablespoons chopped fresh flat-leaf parsley

1 Cook pasta in large saucepan of boiling water
until tender; drain. Cover to keep warm.
2 Meanwhile, cook broccoli and cauliflower in
medium saucepan of boiling water until tender;
drain. Cover to keep warm.
3 Heat oil in same large pan; cook onion, stirring,
until softened. Add mustard, paprika and flour;
cook, stirring, over low heat, 2 minutes. Gradually
stir in milk and soup; stir over heat until mixture
boils and thickens. Add undrained tomatoes;
cook, stirring, until mixture is hot.
4 Preheat grill.
5 Stir pasta, broccoli, cauliflower and 1 cup of
the cheese into tomato mixture; season to taste.
Divide pasta mixture among six 1-cup (250ml)
ovenproof dishes, sprinkle with remaining
cheese; grill until cheese melts and is browned
lightly. Sprinkle pasta bake with parsley just
before serving.

PORK AND VEAL LASAGNE

prep & cook time 1½ hours serves 6 nutritional count per serving 39.3g total fat (20.5g saturated fat); 3428kJ (820 cal); 55.2g carbohydrate; 58.3g protein; 6.3g fibre

1 tablespoon olive oil
1 medium brown onion (150g),
    chopped coarsely
3 trimmed celery stalks (300g),
    chopped coarsely
4 cloves garlic, crushed
2 teaspoons ground cinnamon
800g pork and veal mince (see notes)
1 tablespoon plain flour
2 tablespoons red wine vinegar
2 teaspoons light brown sugar
2⅔ cups (700g) bottled tomato pasta sauce
400g can diced tomatoes
¼ cup finely chopped fresh sage
40g butter
2 tablespoons plain flour, extra
2½ cups (625ml) hot milk
1½ cups (120g) grated parmesan cheese
250g fresh lasagne sheets, trim to fit dish
2½ cups (250g) grated mozzarella cheese
12 fresh sage leaves

1 Heat oil in large pan; cook onion and celery, stirring, until soft. Add garlic and cinnamon; cook, stirring, until fragrant.
2 Add mince to pan; cook, stirring, until meat changes colour. Add flour; cook, stirring, 1 minute. Stir in vinegar, sugar, pasta sauce and undrained tomatoes; bring to the boil. Reduce heat; simmer, stirring occasionally, about 15 minutes or until sauce thickens. Stir in chopped sage; season to taste.
3 Preheat oven to 180°C/160°C fan-forced.
4 Meanwhile, melt butter in medium pan. Add extra flour; cook, stirring, until mixture thickens and bubbles. Gradually stir in milk until mixture boils and thickens. Remove sauce from heat; stir in one-third of the parmesan.
5 Spread a quarter of the meat sauce into shallow 20cm x 30cm ovenproof dish. Cover with one-third of the lasagne sheets, then a third of the remaining meat sauce, half the cheese sauce and half the mozzarella. Make two more layers with the remaining lasagne and meat sauce; top with remaining cheese sauce then sprinkle with combined remaining cheeses. Sprinkle with sage leaves. Bake about 50 minutes or until browned lightly. Stand 10 minutes before serving.

notes Some butchers sell a combined pork and veal mince mixture. If it's not available, use 400g of each. Pizza cheese (375g) can be substituted for the parmesan and mozzarella.
You can make the lasagne a day ahead; put it in the refrigerator and reheat it in the oven (180°C/160°C fan-forced), covered, for about 30 minutes. If you like, freeze the finished lasagne, whole or in serving-sized portions. The whole lasagne will take about 24 hours to thaw in the refrigerator. Individual portions can be thawed in a microwave oven.

BEEF AND EGGPLANT PARMIGIANA LASAGNE

prep & cook time 2¾ hours serves 8 nutritional count per serving 20.9g total fat (8.9g saturated fat); 2123kJ (508 cal); 33.6g carbohydrate; 41g protein; 5.2g fibre

1 tablespoon olive oil
1 medium brown onion (150g), chopped finely
1 clove garlic, crushed
1kg beef mince
½ cup (125ml) dry red wine
2 cups (500ml) beef stock
2⅔ cups (700g) bottled tomato pasta sauce
¼ cup (70g) tomato paste
¾ cup finely chopped fresh basil
2 medium eggplants (600g), peeled,
    sliced thinly
cooking-oil spray
3 fresh lasagne sheets (150g)
2 cups (200g) grated mozzarella cheese
1 cup (100g) packaged breadcrumbs
½ cup (40g) grated parmesan cheese

1 Preheat oven to 200°C/180°C fan-forced.
2 Heat oil in large frying pan; cook onion and garlic, stirring, until onion softens. Add beef; cook, stirring, until browned. Add wine, stock, sauce and paste; bring to the boil, then simmer, covered, 30 minutes, stirring occasionally. Uncover; simmer about 30 minutes or until thickened slightly; stir in basil. Season to taste.
3 Meanwhile, place eggplant on oiled oven tray; spray with oil. Roast about 20 minutes or until tender.
4 Oil shallow 2.5-litre (10-cup) ovenproof dish. Cover base with lasagne sheets, cut to fit; top with about a third of the warm beef mixture, half the eggplant and ⅓ cup mozzarella cheese.
5 Repeat layering with lasagne sheets, another third of the beef mixture, remaining eggplant and ⅓ cup mozzarella cheese, ending with lasagne sheets. Spread remaining third of the beef mixture over lasagne; top with breadcrumbs, parmesan and remaining mozzarella. Bake, covered, in oven, 40 minutes.
6 Preheat grill.
7 Uncover lasagne; cook under grill until browned lightly. Stand 5 minutes before serving.

note Fresh pasta is available from the refrigerated section of most supermarkets. You can use dried pasta instead of fresh, however, you will need to cook the lasagne for at least half an hour longer.

SCALLOPED POTATOES

prep & cook time 1¼ hours serves 6 nutritional count
per serving 28.9g total fat (18.6g saturated fat); 1764kJ
(422 cal); 25.2g carbohydrate; 14.6g protein; 2.7g fibre

Preheat oven to 180°C/160°C fan-forced. Oil
1.5-litre (6-cup) ovenproof dish. Using sharp
knife, mandoline or V-slicer, cut 1.2kg potatoes
into very thin slices; pat dry with absorbent
paper. Finely chop 150g leg ham. Layer a
quarter of the potato into dish; top with a third
of the ham. Continue layering remaining potato
and ham, finishing with potato. Heat 300ml
cream and ¾ cup milk in small saucepan until
almost boiling; pour over potato mixture. Cover
dish with foil; bake in oven 30 minutes. Remove
foil; bake a further 20 minutes. Top with ¾ cup
grated cheddar cheese; bake, uncovered,
about 20 minutes or until potato is tender.
Stand 10 minutes before serving.

POTATOES WITH CREAM

prep & cook time 1½ hours serves 4 nutritional count
per serving 33g total fat (21.6g saturated fat); 2006kJ
(480 cal); 35.2g carbohydrate; 9.3g protein; 4.1g fibre

Preheat oven to 180°C/160°C fan-forced. Oil
deep 19cm-square cake pan. Layer 1.2kg thinly
sliced peeled potatoes in pan; sprinkle with a
pinch of ground nutmeg. Pour 1 cup cream
over potatoes; sprinkle with ¼ cup grated
parmesan cheese. Dot top with 20g chopped
butter. Bake, covered, in oven, 30 minutes.
Uncover; bake about 45 minutes or until
potatoes are tender and top is browned lightly.

POTATO BAKES

CREAMED POTATOES WITH ROSEMARY AND CHEESE

prep & cook time 1½ hours serves 6 nutritional count per serving 12g total fat (7.8g saturated fat); 686kJ (164 cal); 10.1g carbohydrate; 3.5g protein; 11.2g fibre

Preheat oven to 180°C/160°C fan-forced. Oil 2.5-litre (10-cup) ovenproof dish. Using sharp knife, mandoline or V-slicer, cut 1kg potatoes into thin slices; pat dry with absorbent paper. Combine 300ml cream, 2 crushed garlic cloves, 1 tablespoon finely chopped fresh rosemary and 2 crumbled chicken stock cubes in small bowl. Layer a quarter of the potato, slightly overlapping, in dish; top with a quarter of the cream mixture. Continue layering with potato and cream mixture. Press potato firmly with spatula to completely submerge in cream, cover dish with foil; bake 1 hour. Remove foil; sprinkle with ½ cup grated parmesan cheese. Bake a further 20 minutes or until potato is tender and cheese browns lightly.

POTATOES BYRON

prep & cook time 1¼ hours serves 4 nutritional count per serving 30.2g total fat (19.7g saturated fat); 1910kJ (457 cal); 33.8g carbohydrate; 10.8g protein; 5g fibre

Preheat oven to 180°C/160°C fan-forced. Oil four 1-cup (250ml) ovenproof dishes. Pierce skins of 1kg unpeeled potatoes with fork; place on oven tray. Bake about 1 hour or until tender. Cover; cool 10 minutes. Increase oven temperature to 220°C/200°C fan-forced. Split potatoes in half lengthways; scoop flesh into medium bowl, discard potato skins. Mash potato with 60g chopped butter. Divide mashed potato among dishes, smooth tops; do not pack mixture down tightly. Pour ½ cup cream evenly over dishes; sprinkle with combined ¼ cup grated parmesan cheese and ¼ cup grated gruyère cheese. Bake, in oven, about 10 minutes or until heated through and browned lightly.

JANSSEN'S TEMPTATION

prep & cook time **1½ hours** serves **4** nutritional count
per serving **26.5g total fat (17.1g saturated fat); 1868kJ
(447 cal); 39.2g carbohydrate; 10.5g protein; 6g fibre**

Preheat oven to 220°C/200°C fan-forced. Grease
medium deep 22cm-square baking dish. Thinly
slice 1kg potatoes and 1 large brown onion. Halve
9 drained anchovy fillets. Layer a third of the
potato over base of dish; sprinkle over a third
of the onion and a third of the anchovy. Sprinkle
with 1 tablespoon lemon juice. Repeat layering
two more times with potato, onion, anchovy
and juice. Pour over ¾ cup cream; sprinkle
2 tablespoons each stale breadcrumbs and
chopped fresh flat-leaf parsley over top then
dot with 30g butter. Bake, covered, about
1 hour or until potato is tender. Uncover; bake
about 15 minutes or until browned lightly.

note **This is our take on the traditional Swedish recipe
of the same name.**

KUMARA, BACON AND EGG BAKE

prep & cook time **1 hour** serves **4** nutritional count
per serving **31.7g total fat (15.6g saturated fat); 2195kJ
(525 cal); 18.1g carbohydrate; 41.1g protein; 2.4g fibre**

Preheat oven to 180°C/160°C fan-forced. Grease
2.5 litre (10-cup) baking dish. Boil, steam or
microwave 1 thinly sliced large kumara for
5 minutes. Drain; pat dry with absorbent paper.
Place in a single layer over base of dish; sprinkle
with ½ teaspoon ground cumin. Meanwhile,
cook 5 finely chopped rindless bacon rashers
and 1 finely chopped medium brown onion in
heated medium frying pan, stirring, until onion
softens. Stir in ½ teaspoon ground cumin;
spread mixture over kumara. Whisk 8 eggs,
¼ cup cream and 1 cup grated cheddar cheese
in medium bowl; season. Pour egg mixture
over kumara. Bake about 30 minutes or until
browned lightly.

SIMPLE BAKES

TOMATO AND BEAN BAKE

prep & cook time **40 minutes** serves **4** nutritional count per serving **12.5g total fat (5.2g saturated fat); 1195kJ (286 cal); 22.4g carbohydrate; 17g protein; 8g fibre**

Heat 2 teaspoons olive oil in medium pan; cook 1 chopped small brown onion and 100g chopped trimmed green beans. Add a 420g can rinsed, drained four-bean mix, 250g halved cherry tomatoes, 2 tablespoons tomato paste and ½ cup water; cook until tomato softens. Preheat grill. Combine 2 teaspoons olive oil, 90g chopped wholemeal bread and ½ cup pizza cheese in small bowl. Stir 2 tablespoons chopped fresh basil into bean mixture. Spoon bean mixture into four 1-cup (250ml) shallow ovenproof dishes, top with bread mixture. Grill until bread is brown and crisp.

CHICKEN SPINACH CANNELLONI

prep & cook time **35 minutes** serves **4** nutritional count per serving **16g total fat (7.8g saturated fat); 1848kJ (442 cal); 38.6g carbohydrate; 32.4g protein; 5.7g fibre**

Preheat oven to 220°C/200°C fan-forced. Combine 1½ cups shredded barbecued chicken, 250g coarsely chopped, thawed frozen spinach and 200g ricotta cheese in medium bowl, season. Spoon mixture into 12 cannelloni tubes. Spread 1⅓ cups bottled tomato pasta sauce into four small shallow ovenproof dishes; place cannelloni, in single layer, on top of sauce. Pour 1⅓ cups bottled tomato pasta sauce over cannelloni; sprinkle with ¾ cup coarsely grated pizza cheese. Cover cannelloni with foil; bake about 25 minutes or until pasta is tender.

note **You need to buy half a large (450g) barbecued chicken for this recipe.**

PEPITA AND OAK LEAF SALAD

prep time **10 minutes** serves **6** nutritional count
per serving **9.8g total fat (0.9g saturated fat); 464kJ
(111 cal); 4.4g carbohydrate; 0.7g protein; 2g fibre**

Combine 2 tablespoons each of olive oil, red
wine vinegar and cranberry sauce in screw-top
jar; shake well, season to taste. Separate the
leaves from 1 green oak lettuce. Combine
lettuce, 1/3 cup roasted pepitas and 1 thinly
sliced small red onion in medium bowl with
dressing; toss gently.

COS, AVOCADO AND TOMATO SALAD

prep time **15 minutes** serves **4** nutritional count
per serving **20.2g total fat (4.3g saturated fat); 970kJ
(232 cal); 5.8g carbohydrate; 4.3g protein; 4.8g fibre**

Separate leaves from 1 baby cos lettuce; shred
leaves coarsely. Combine lettuce with 3 finely
chopped medium tomatoes, 2 finely chopped
medium avocadoes, 1 finely chopped lebanese
cucumber, 1 finely chopped small red onion,
1/4 cup coarsely chopped fresh coriander, 1/4 cup
lime juice and 2 crushed garlic cloves in large
bowl; season to taste.

GREEN BEAN, TOMATO AND HAZELNUT SALAD

prep & cook time **20 minutes** serves **4** nutritional count
per serving **20.2g total fat (1.8g saturated fat); 920kJ
(220 cal); 3.6g carbohydrate; 4.2g protein; 4.3g fibre**

Combine 1/2 cup coarsely chopped roasted
hazelnuts, 1 teaspoon wholegrain mustard,
2 tablespoons each of hazelnut oil and cider
vinegar in screw-top jar; shake well, season
to taste. Boil, steam or microwave 200g green
beans until tender; drain. Rinse under cold
water; drain. Combine beans, 250g halved
cherry tomatoes and dressing in medium bowl;
toss gently.

PEAR, WALNUT AND FETTA SALAD

prep time **20 minutes** serves **4** nutritional count
per serving **16.6g total fat (5g saturated fat); 957kJ
(229 cal); 10.4g carbohydrate; 8.4g protein; 3.3g fibre**

Place 1 tablespoon walnut oil, 2 tablespoons
white wine vinegar, 1 tablespoon finely chopped
fresh chives and 2 teaspoons wholegrain
mustard in screw-top jar; shake well, season
to taste. Separate leaves of 1 butter lettuce;
tear leaves roughly. Slice 1 medium unpeeled,
cored pear into thin wedges. Combine lettuce,
pear, 1/3 cup coarsely chopped roasted walnuts,
40g trimmed snow pea sprouts, 50g crumbled
fetta, 35g shaved parmesan cheese and dressing
in large bowl; toss gently.

note **Use any pear you like in this salad, as long as it's
firm, crunchy and holds its shape when cut.**

SIMPLE SIDE SALADS

OAK LEAF, MIXED HERB AND DIJON SALAD

prep time **10 minutes** serves **6** nutritional count per serving **6.2g total fat (0.9g saturated fat); 288kJ (69 cal); 2g carbohydrate; 0.7g protein; 1.1g fibre**

Combine 2 tablespoons each of olive oil and white wine vinegar, 1 tablespoon dijon mustard and 2 teaspoons white sugar in screw-top jar; shake well, season to taste. Separate leaves of 1 green oak leaf lettuce; combine lettuce, ¼ cup coarsely chopped fresh chives, ½ cup each of firmly packed fresh flat-leaf parsley leaves and fresh chervil leaves in medium bowl with dressing; toss gently.

ORANGE AND DATE COUSCOUS

prep time **15 minutes** serves **4** nutritional count per serving **5.1g total fat (0.7g saturated fat); 1329kJ (318 cal); 56.7g carbohydrate; 8.2g protein; 4.9g fibre**

Combine 1 cup couscous with 1 cup boiling water in medium heatproof bowl, cover; stand about 5 minutes or until water is absorbed, fluffing with fork occasionally. Meanwhile, coarsely grate rind from 2 medium oranges. Segment oranges over small bowl; reserve any juice in bowl (you need ¼ cup juice). Stir orange segments, reserved juice, 40g baby spinach leaves, ½ thinly sliced small red onion, ½ cup thinly sliced seeded fresh dates and 1 tablespoon olive oil into couscous; season to taste.

ROCKET, PARMESAN AND SEMI-DRIED TOMATO SALAD

prep time **10 minutes** serves **4** nutritional count per serving **12.3g total fat (2.3g saturated fat); 635kJ (152 cal); 4.4g carbohydrate; 5.1g protein; 2.2g fibre**

Combine 1 tablespoon each of balsamic vinegar and olive oil, 100g baby rocket leaves, 2 tablespoons roasted pine nuts, 40g coarsely chopped drained semi-dried tomatoes and ⅓ cup flaked parmesan cheese in large bowl; toss gently, season to taste.

MIXED LEAF SALAD WITH CRANBERRY DRESSING

prep time **15 minutes** serves **8** nutritional count per serving **10.1g total fat (1.2g saturated fat); 619kJ (148 cal); 10.7g carbohydrate; 2.8g protein; 2.4g fibre**

Combine ¼ cup each of olive oil and red wine vinegar, 2 tablespoons each of cranberry juice and cranberry sauce, 2 teaspoons dijon mustard, 1 crushed garlic clove and ½ finely chopped small red onion in screw-top jar; shake well, season to taste. Separate leaves of 1 baby cos lettuce and 1 small radicchio. Combine lettuce and radicchio with 250g trimmed rocket in large serving bowl; sprinkle with ½ cup flaked almonds and ½ cup dried cranberries, drizzle with dressing.

BACON, SHORTCUT is a "half rasher"; the streaky (belly), narrow portion of the rasher has been removed leaving the choice cut eye meat (fat end).

BASIL an aromatic herb; there are many types, but the most commonly used is sweet, or common, basil.

BAY LEAVES aromatic leaves from the bay tree; used to flavour soups, stocks and casseroles.

BEANS

broad also known as fava, windsor and horse beans; available dried, fresh, canned and frozen. Fresh and frozen forms should be peeled twice, discarding both the outer long green pod and the beige-green tough inner shell.

four-bean mix is made up of kidney beans, butter beans, chickpeas and cannellini beans.

white some recipes in this book may simply call for "white beans", a generic term used for canned or dried cannellini, haricot, navy or great northern beans all of which can be substituted for the other.

BREADCRUMBS, STALE one- or two-day-old bread made into crumbs by grating, blending or processing.

BUTTERMILK originally the term given to the slightly sour liquid left after butter was churned from cream, today it is commercially made similarly to yogurt. It is sold alongside all fresh milk products in supermarkets. Despite the implication of its name, buttermilk is low in fat.

CAPSICUM also known as bell pepper or pepper. Native to Central and South America, they can be red, green, yellow, orange or purplish black. Discard seeds and membranes before use.

CAYENNE PEPPER see chilli.

CELERIAC tuberous root with brown skin, white flesh and a celery-like flavour.

CHEESE

cheddar the most common cows'-milk "tasty" cheese; should be aged, hard and have a pronounced bite.

fontina a smooth firm cheese with a nutty taste and a brown or red rind.

gorgonzola a creamy molded Italian blue cheese having a mild, sweet taste.

gruyère a Swiss cheese having small holes and a nutty, slightly salty, flavour.

mozzarella soft, spun-curd cheese; traditionally made from water buffalo milk, though cows'-milk versions are now available. It has a low melting point and wonderfully elastic texture when heated and is used to add texture rather than flavour.

parmesan also known as parmigiano; is a hard, grainy cows'-milk cheese originating in the Parma region of Italy. The curd is salted in brine for a month before being aged for up to two years in humid conditions.

pecorino the generic Italian name for cheeses made from sheep milk. It's a hard, white to pale yellow cheese.

pizza a commercial blend of varying proportions of processed grated mozzarella, cheddar and parmesan cheeses.

CHICKPEAS also called channa, garbanzos or hummus; a round, sandy-coloured legume.

CHILLI available in many different types and sizes. Use rubber gloves when seeding and chopping fresh chillies as they can burn your skin. Removing seeds and membranes lessens the heat level.

cayenne pepper a long, thin-fleshed, extremely hot red chilli usually sold dried and ground.

flakes deep-red dehydrated very fine slices and whole seeds.

green any unripened chilli and some that are green when ripe.

long red available both fresh and dried; a generic term used for any moderately hot, long (6cm-8cm) thin chilli.

red thai small, hot and bright red in colour.

CHORIZO a sausage of Spanish origin, which is made of coarsely ground pork, highly seasoned with garlic and chillies.

CORIANDER also known as pak chee, cilantro or chinese parsley; bright-green leafy herb with a pungent flavour. Both the stems and roots of coriander are also used in Thai cooking; wash well before using. Also available ground or as seeds; these should not be substituted for fresh coriander as the tastes are completely different.

GLOSSARY

COUSCOUS a fine, grain-like cereal product made from semolina; a dough of semolina flour and water is sieved then dehydrated to produce minuscule even-sized pellets; couscous is rehydrated by steaming, or with the addition of a warm liquid, and swells to three times its original size.

CUMIN a spice also known as zeera or comino; has a spicy, nutty flavour.

EGGPLANT also known as aubergine; belongs to the same family as tomatoes, chillies and potatoes. Ranging in size from tiny to very large and in colour from pale green to deep purple, eggplant has an equally wide variety of flavours.

FENNEL BULB also known as finocchio or anise; a white to very pale green, firm, crisp, roundish vegetable about 8-12cm in diameter. The bulb has a slightly sweet, anise flavour but the leaves have a much stronger taste.

FIRM WHITE FISH FILLET blue eye, bream, flathead, swordfish, ling, whiting, jewfish or snapper are all good choices. Check for any small pieces of bone in the fillets and use tweezers to remove them.

FLOUR, PLAIN an all-purpose flour made from wheat.

GNOCCHI Italian "dumplings" made from potatoes, semolina or flour; cooked in boiling water or baked with cheese or sauce.

KUMARA Polynesian name of an orange-fleshed sweet potato often confused with yam.

LENTILS (red, brown, yellow) dried pulses often identified by and named after their colour.

french-style green lentils related to the famous french lentils du puy; these green-blue, tiny lentils have a nutty, earthy flavour and a hardy nature that allows them to be rapidly cooked without disintegrating. Are also known as australian, bondi or matilda lentils.

LETTUCE

butter have small, round, loosely formed heads with soft, buttery-textured leaves ranging from pale green on the outer leaves to pale yellow-green on the inner leaves. Has a sweet flavour.

cos also known as romaine lettuce; the traditional caesar salad lettuce. Long, with leaves ranging from dark green on the outside to almost white near the core; the leaves have a stiff centre rib that gives a slight cupping effect to the leaf on either side.

iceberg a heavy, firm round lettuce with tightly packed leaves and a crisp texture.

lamb's also known as mâche, corn salad or lamb tongue; the tender narrow dark-green leaves have a mild, almost nutty flavour.

oak leaf also known as Feuille de Chene. Available in both red and green leaf.

wombok also known as peking cabbage, chinese cabbage or petsai. Elongated in shape with pale green, crinkly leaves, this is the most common cabbage in South-East Asian cooking. Can be eaten raw or cooked.

MERGUEZ a small, spicy sausage that is believed to have originated in Tunisia but is eaten throughout North Africa and Spain. Merguez is traditionally made with lamb meat and is easily recognised because of its chilli-red colour. Merguez can be found in many butchers, delicatessens and sausage specialty stores.

MINCE also known as ground meat, as in beef, veal, lamb, pork and chicken.

MUSTARD

dijon a pale brown, distinctively flavoured, mild French mustard.

wholegrain also known as seeded. A French-style coarse-grain mustard made from crushed mustard seeds and dijon-style french mustard.

OIL

olive made from ripened olives. Extra virgin and virgin are the best, while extra light or light refers to taste, not fat levels.

peanut pressed from ground peanuts; most commonly used oil in Asian cooking because of its high smoke point (capacity to handle high heat without burning).

vegetable sourced from plants rather than animal fats.

ONIONS

brown and white these onions are interchangeable, however, the white onion has a more pungent flesh.

green also known as scallion or, incorrectly, shallot; an immature onion picked before the bulb has formed, having a long, bright-green edible stalk.

shallot also called french shallots, golden shallots or eschalots; small, elongated, brown-skinned members of the onion family. Grows in tight clusters similar to garlic.

spring these onions have small white bulbs and long narrow green-leafed tops.

red also known as spanish, red spanish or bermuda onion; a large, sweet-flavoured, purple-red onion.

OREGANO a herb, also known as wild marjoram; has a woody stalk with tiny, dark green leaves that have a pungent, peppery flavour and are used fresh or dried.

PANCETTA an Italian bacon that is cured, but not smoked.

PAPRIKA ground dried sweet red capsicum (bell pepper); there are many types available, including sweet, hot, mild and smoked.

PARSLEY, FLAT-LEAF also known as continental or italian parsley.

POLENTA also known as cornmeal; a flour-like cereal made of dried corn (maize) sold ground in several different textures; also the name of the dish made from it.

PROSCIUTTO cured, air-dried (unsmoked), pressed ham.

ROCKET also known as arugula, rugula and rucola; a peppery-tasting green leaf used similarly to baby spinach leaves, eaten raw in salad or used in cooking. Baby rocket leaves are both smaller and less peppery.

SILVER BEET also known as swiss chard and, mistakenly, spinach; a member of the beet family grown for its tasty green leaves and celery-like stems.

SNOW PEA SPROUTS tender new growths of snow peas; also known as mange tout.

SPINACH also known as english spinach and, incorrectly, silver beet. Baby spinach leaves are also available.

SPLIT PEAS a variety of yellow or green pea grown specifically for drying. When dried, the peas usually split along a natural seam. Whole and split dried peas are available packaged in supermarkets and in bulk in health-food stores.

SUGAR

brown a soft, finely granulated sugar retaining molasses for its colour and flavour.

caster also known as superfine or finely granulated table sugar.

white a granulated table sugar, also known as crystal sugar.

SWEDE known in Scotland as the traditional accompaniment to haggis. Stronger and sweeter in flavour than the turnip, it is easy to identify by its purple-hued, creamy-coloured skin and flesh.

TOMATO

canned whole peeled tomatoes in natural juices; available diced, crushed or chopped, sometimes unsalted or reduced salt. Used in recipes with the juice (undrained).

egg also called plum or roma tomato; smallish, oval-shaped tomatoes much used in Italian cooking or salads.

pasta sauce a prepared sauce made from a blend of tomatoes, herbs and spices.

paste triple-concentrated tomato puree used to flavour soups, stews, sauces and casseroles.

puree canned pureed tomatoes (not tomato paste). Substitute with fresh peeled pureed tomato.

semi-dried partially dried tomato pieces in olive oil; softer and juicier than sun-dried, these are not a preserve so they do not keep as long as sun-dried.

TREVALLY thick, moist, white-fleshed fish.

TURNIP is similar to swede and the two are often confused, but the turnip's skin and flesh are whiter in colour. Its leafy green tops can be washed, trimmed and used like spinach.

VINEGAR

balsamic made from the juice of Trebbiano grapes; it is a deep rich brown colour with a sweet and sour flavour. It ranges in pungency and quality depending on how long it's been aged. Quality can be determined up to a point by price; use the most expensive sparingly.

cider (apple cider) made from fermented apples.

raspberry made from fresh raspberries steeped in a white wine vinegar.

red wine based on fermented red wine.

white wine made from a blend of white wines.

WATERCRESS also known as winter rocket. Belongs to the cress family, a large group of peppery greens. Highly perishable, so must be used as soon as possible after purchase.

ZUCCHINI a small green, yellow or white vegetable belonging to the squash family; also known as courgette.

CONVERSION CHART

MEASURES

One Australian metric measuring cup holds approximately 250ml, one Australian metric tablespoon holds 20ml, one Australian metric teaspoon holds 5ml.

The difference between one country's measuring cups and another's is within a 2- or 3-teaspoon variance, and will not affect your cooking results. North America, New Zealand and the United Kingdom use a 15ml tablespoon. All cup and spoon measurements are level. The most accurate way of measuring dry ingredients is to weigh them. When measuring liquids, use a clear glass or plastic jug with metric markings.

We use large eggs with an average weight of 60g.

DRY MEASURES

METRIC	IMPERIAL
15g	½oz
30g	1oz
60g	2oz
90g	3oz
125g	4oz (¼lb)
155g	5oz
185g	6oz
220g	7oz
250g	8oz (½lb)
280g	9oz
315g	10oz
345g	11oz
375g	12oz (¾lb)
410g	13oz
440g	14oz
470g	15oz
500g	16oz (1lb)
750g	24oz (1½lb)
1kg	32oz (2lb)

LIQUID MEASURES

METRIC	IMPERIAL
30ml	1 fluid oz
60ml	2 fluid oz
100ml	3 fluid oz
125ml	4 fluid oz
150ml	5 fluid oz
190ml	6 fluid oz
250ml	8 fluid oz
300ml	10 fluid oz
500ml	16 fluid oz
600ml	20 fluid oz
1000ml (1 litre)	1¾ pints

LENGTH MEASURES

METRIC	IMPERIAL
3mm	⅛in
6mm	¼in
1cm	½in
2cm	¾in
2.5cm	1in
5cm	2in
6cm	2½in
8cm	3in
10cm	4in
13cm	5in
15cm	6in
18cm	7in
20cm	8in
23cm	9in
25cm	10in
28cm	11in
30cm	12in (1ft)

OVEN TEMPERATURES

These oven temperatures are only a guide for conventional ovens.
For fan-forced ovens, check the manufacturer's manual.

	°C (CELSIUS)	°F (FAHRENHEIT)	GAS MARK
Very slow	120	250	½
Slow	150	275-300	1-2
Moderately slow	160	325	3
Moderate	180	350-375	4-5
Moderately hot	200	400	6
Hot	220	425-450	7-8
Very hot	240	475	9

INDEX

Published in 2010 by ACP Books, Sydney
ACP Books are published by ACP Magazines
a division of PBL Media Pty Limited

ACP BOOKS

General manager Christine Whiston
Editor-in-chief Susan Tomnay
Creative director Hieu Chi Nguyen
Art director Hannah Blackmore
Designer Sarah Holmes
Senior editor Wendy Bryant
Food director Pamela Clark
Food editor Rebecca Squadrito

Sales & rights director Brian Cearnes
Marketing manager Bridget Cody
Senior business analyst Rebecca Varela
Circulation manager Jama Mclean
Operations manager David Scotto
Production manager Victoria Jefferys

**Published by ACP Books, a division of
ACP Magazines Ltd, 54 Park St, Sydney;
GPO Box 4088, Sydney, NSW 2001.
phone (02) 9282 8618; fax (02) 9267 9438.
acpbooks@acpmagazines.com.au;
www.acpbooks.com.au**

Printed by Toppan Printing Co., China.

United Kingdom Distributed by Australian Consolidated Press (UK),
phone (01604) 642 200; fax (01604) 642 300; books@acpuk.com

Title: Gratins & bakes / food director Pamela Clark.
ISBN: 978 186396 932 1 (pbk.)
Notes: Includes index.
Subjects: Baking. Casserole cookery.
Other Authors/Contributors: Clark, Pamela.
Dewey Number: 641.71© ACP Magazines Ltd 2010
ABN 18 053 273 546

Cover Cauliflower gratin, page 21
Photographer Stuart Scott
Stylist Kate Brown
Food preparation Rebecca Squadrito

Send recipe enquiries to: recipeenquiries@acpmagazines.com.au